The Box of Delights

Piers Torday began his career in theatre and then television as a producer and writer. His first book for children, *The Last Wild*, was shortlisted for the Waterstones Children's Book Prize. The sequel, *The Dark Wild*, won the Guardian Children's Fiction Prize. Other books include *The Wild Beyond*, *There May Be a Castle*, *The Death of an Owl* (with Paul Torday), *The Lost Magician* (Teach Primary Award), *The Frozen Sea* and *The Wild Before*. His plays include *The Box of Delights* (Wilton's Music Hall/RSC), *Christmas Carol: A Fairy Tale*, *The Child in the Snow* and *Wind in the Wilton's* (Wilton's Music Hall). His book *There May Be a Castle* was adapted for the stage by Barb Jungr and Samantha Lane for Little Angel Theatre. He is a Trustee of the Unicorn Theatre, an Artistic Associate at Wilton's Music Hall, and lives in London.

John Masefield (1878–1967) was the fifteenth Poet Laureate, and author of over sixty-two collections of poetry, twenty-three plays, seventeen novels and seven books for children, among other work. His poetry includes 'Sea-Fever', 'Cargoes', *The Everlasting Mercy*, *Salt-Water Ballads* and *Reynard the Fox*. Among his plays are *The Campden Wonder*, *The Tragedy of Pompey the Great* and *Good Friday*. Books for children include *A Book of Discoveries*, *The Midnight Folk* and *The Box of Delights or When the Wolves Were Running*, which has been adapted several times for radio and television, and received its world premiere on stage at Wilton's Music Hall in 2017. Masefield was awarded the Order of Merit in 1937, and was the first president of the Society of Authors. His ashes are buried in Poets Corner at Westminster Abbey.

PIERS TORDAY

The Box of Delights

based on the novel by
JOHN MASEFIELD

faber

First published in 2017
by Faber and Faber Limited
The Bindery, 51 Hatton Garden
London, EC1N 8HN

Published in this edition in 2023

Typeset by Brighton Gray
Printed and bound in the UK by CPI Group (Ltd), Croydon CR0 4YY

All rights reserved
© Piers Torday, 2023

Piers Torday is hereby identified as author
of this work in accordance with Section 77 of the
Copyright, Designs and Patents Act 1988

All rights whatsoever in this work, amateur or professional, are
strictly reserved. Applications for permission for any use whatsoever,
including performance rights, must be made in advance, prior to
any such proposed use, to Curtis Brown Group Ltd,
Cunard House, 15 Regent Street, London SW1Y 4LR

No performance may be given unless a licence
has first been obtained

This book is sold subject to the condition that it shall not,
by way of trade or otherwise, be lent, resold, hired out
or otherwise circulated without the publisher's prior consent
in any form of binding or cover other than that in which
it is published and without a similar condition including
this condition being imposed on the subsequent purchaser

A CIP record for this book
is available from the British Library

978-0-571-39015-1

Printed and bound in the UK on FSC® certified paper in line with our continuing
commitment to ethical business practices, sustainability and the environment.
For further information see faber.co.uk/environmental-policy

Our authorised representative in the EU for product safety is
Easy Access System Europe, Mustamäe tee 50, 10621 Tallinn, Estonia
gpsr.requests@easproject.com

4 6 8 10 9 7 5

The Box of Delights:
Making a Christmas Classic

The midwinter has always been a natural time for storytelling. Our ancestors gathered around fires and shared tales of heroes and hope to banish the cold and the dark away.

That tradition has given us many classic stories that we enjoy sharing year after year while we decorate trees, feast and exchange gifts. A story about the possibility of redemptive change as the year turns, such as *A Christmas Carol*, or a story about the healing power of family love like *Little Women*, or perhaps simply the enchanting magic of a child's imagination at winter in *The Snowman*.

But how did John Masefield's *Box of Delights* become one of those stories that countless fans read with their family yearly or enjoy through the classic BBC adaptation?

Quite simply, because there is no other story like it. It is a vision of imagination, wonder and endless excitement in a class of its own.

John Masefield published his first poem during the reign of Queen Victoria, but one of his final works was a poem on the assassination of JFK. He witnessed the extraordinary, tumultuous change of the early twentieth century, and few children's books speak as much to the traditions of the past whilst also wholeheartedly embracing the future. Masefield drew on the folklore of his Victorian childhood to conjure up a half-world of prowling wolves in the snowy shadows, antlered gods and muttering statues. But the book is also packed with bang-up-to-date thrills for his time – criminal gangs, machine guns, telephones, aeroplanes . . . and time travel.

Many stories are set around Christmas, but few are so preoccupied with saving the Christmas festival as this one. As a child, Masefield's bedroom looked out onto his local church.

When he watched the clergy process in and out in their finery, he idly wondered what would happen if they were all kidnapped – or 'scrobbled'. What *would* it take to cancel Christmas?

Several keystone texts of British children's fantasy followed *The Box of Delights* – but it was the first with so many ideas now enshrined in our cultural imagination. Before Lucy Pevensie discovered that opening a wardrobe could lead to Narnia in C. S. Lewis's *The Lion, the Witch and the Wardrobe*, Kay Harker opened a box and found a world of wonder. Before J. R. R. Tolkien ever imagined Gandalf the Grey in a wizarding duel with Saruman the White in *Lord of the Rings*, Cole Hawlings and Abner Brown were locked in combat over magical powers. And before the Weasleys ever revved their airborne Flying Ford Anglia in J. K. Rowling's *Harry Potter and the Chamber of Secrets*, Sylvia Daisy Pouncer took to the skies in her Car-o-Plane.

But most of all, this is a deeply good book by a remarkable human. John Masefield, whom Muriel Spark described in her critical study as almost looking like Santa Claus – 'a lovely looking old man, with rosy cheeks, pure white hair and moustache and blue blue eyes' – was also 'unaffectedly gracious, kind and sweet'. His lasting seasonal gift to us was this story of imagination and hope. A story that does not preach or sentimentalise, but instead, with endless invention, wit and generosity, shows us all that when the wolves run, if we believe in each other and dare to dream the impossible – we might just escape their bite.

Piers Torday

The Box of Delights, a Wilton's Music Hall and Hero Productions Commission, was first performed at Wilton's Music Hall, London, on 1 December 2017. The cast, in alphabetical order, was as follows:

Bishop of Tatchester / Train Conductor Mark Extance
Sylvia Daisy Pouncer / Caroline Louisa Josefina Gabrielle
Maria Jones Safiyya Ingar
Charles / Inspector of Police Tom Kanji
Cole Hawlings / Abner Brown Matthew Kelly
Peter Jones Samuel Simmonds
Herne the Hunter / Rat / Abner's Head Rosalind Steele
Kay Harker Alastair Toovey

Director Justin Audibert
Designer Tom Piper
Lighting Designer Anna Watson
Composer and Sound Designer Ed Lewis
Video Designer Nina Dunn
Movement Director Simon Pittman
Puppetry Designer Samuel Wyer
Casting Director Vicky Richardson

The Box of Delights was revived at the Royal Shakespeare Theatre, Stratford-upon-Avon, on 31 October 2023. The cast, in alphabetical order, was as follows:

Joe / Ensemble Nana Amoo-Gottfried
Kay Harker Callum Balmforth
Cole Hawlings / Grandad Stephen Boxer
Mayor / Ensemble Melody Brown
Ensemble / Puppeteer Alex Cardall
Rat / Puppeteer Tom Chapman
Herne the Hunter Janet Etuk
Sylvia Daisy Pouncer Nia Gwynne
Peter Jones Jack Humphrey
Charles Tom Kanji
Abner Brown Richard Lynch
Caroline Louisa Annette McLaughlin
Maria Jones Mae Munuo
Sylvia Daisy Pouncer Claire Price
Ellen / The Head / Ensemble Molly Roberts
Ensemble / Puppeteer Rhiannon Skerritt
Bishop / Ensemble Timothy Speyer
Papergirl / Duchess of Musborough / Ensemble Rosie Wyatt

All other parts played by members of the company

Director Justin Audibert
Designer Tom Piper
Lighting Prema Mehta
Music Ed Lewis
Sound Claire Windsor
Movement Simon Pittman

Video Nina Dunn & Matthew Brown
Puppetry Samuel Wyer
Fights Kev McCurdy
Dramaturg Réjane Collard-Walker
Music Director Ben McQuigg
Voice and Text Stephen Kemble
Associate Director Hannah Joss
Associate Designer Fran Norburn
Assistant Director Thyrza Abrahams
Casting Director Matthew Dewsbury CDG
Head of New Work Pippa Hill
Producers Sarah-Katy Davies, Zoë Donegan

Characters

Christmas, Now

Grandad
Kay Harker, his grandson, twelve

Christmas, Then

Train Conductor
Cole Hawlings, a showman
Barney, a Toby dog
Charles
Joe
Abner Brown
Sylvia Daisy Pouncer
Caroline Louisa, Kay's guardian
Maria Jones, Caroline's other ward
Peter Jones, her brother
Butcher
Grocer
Baker
Herne the Hunter, a goddess
A Phoenix
Ramon
Ellen, a maid
The Bishop of Tatchester
The Mayor of Tatchester
Rat
The Duchess of Musborough
Papergirl
The Head, a magical talking sculpture
Cathedral Choir: Dean, Canon Rector and **Precentor**

THE BOX OF DELIGHTS

Act One

SCENE ONE: THE STRANGEST DREAM

Christmas Eve, modern day. The attic of Seekings House. Cupboards and trunks under dustsheets . . . an old painting . . . a world of muted, real-life greyness.

A key echoes in a lock . . . a tiny attic corner door opens, admitting a shaft of light. Grandad totters in behind his grandson Kay, who wields a torch.

Grandad Look at all this, Kay. The Harker inheritance!

Kay Is it worth millions?

Grandad A value beyond mere money to those who know.

Kay Whatever.

Grandad Something to show you. Cheer you up. As you're stuck here for Christmas with boring old Grandad –

Kay – I never said that. You don't need to worry about me –

Grandad – I'm not! Want to see it for myself, too – one last time.

Kay waves some dust out of the air.

Not been up here for years.

Kay I can see why.

Grandad Too many memories!

He sits down with a thump on an old trunk, wheezing.

Kay Or maybe just the stairs.

Grandad Or maybe just the stairs!

Beat.

Come on, sit. Let me catch my breath.

Kay sits next to him. Awkward pause.

Grandad Someone's very quiet today.

Kay I'm fine.

Grandad Come on. I'm not daft.

Kay It's nothing! (*Trying to change the subject.*) What did you want to show me, anyway?

Grandad Kay. If this is about Mum and Dad –

Kay – No!

Grandad – You can talk to me. I won't tell, honest.

Kay It's nothing . . . I mean, it's just . . . I don't know . . . you're gonna think I'm . . . but, what about . . . Christmas?

Grandad What about it? You've seen the tree, I've ordered the turkey, there are mince pies galore . . . you and me, your mum – when she gets here – we'll have a cracking time. Can't wait!

Kay I don't mean that! I mean . . . will it be the same?

Grandad It'll be different. You and Mum are coming to me this year, you to your dad next year. They'll make it special, trust me.

Kay But what if they don't?

Grandad You have to give them some time. Kay, this Christmas isn't the first time the wolves have been running.

Kay I haven't seen any wolves. Not in Coventry, anyway.

Grandad Do you ever dream, Kay?

Kay Everyone says I daydream too much. Teachers. Dad.

Grandad Runs in the family. I used to dream, too. So many dreams. The sign of a strong imagination.

Kay And what good is that?

Grandad Never say that! Never. It's all the good in the world.

Kay Doesn't change anything, though, does it?

Grandad You could not be more wrong.
I'll show you.

Kay helps him up. They explore one of the crates under a sheet. Kay finds a 1930s stuffed dog toy and a vintage toy racing car. A train set!

Ah. This will shed some light on it for you.

The lights in the train flicker on.

Kay Grandad! Look! It's working!

The train coils up into the air like an articulated serpent, growing, becoming bigger, louder, brighter –

What's happening?

Grandad Like you, Kay, I have always dreamed. But no dream was as strange –

A loud rattle of wheels as the train spins around to fly straight at us –

As the one I had that Christmas!

Steam clouds explode around Kay with dazzling lights as Seekings and Grandad vanish in the roar of a train engine –

SCENE TWO: A LITTLE CARD TRICK

Christmas, before the war. A packed steam train rattles through frosted, overgrown embankments and down dark tunnels. Kay is curled up, fast asleep.
Spiky silhouettes of castles and woods flicker past.

Conductor Tickets, please! Tickets for Condicote and Tatchester from Musborough Junction!

A Dog appears, like the stuffed dog from before. He paws at Kay, trying to wake him up.

Kay (*stirring*) Hello, boy! Where did you come from?

Conductor Tickets, please, young man.

Kay (*to Dog*) Good thing you woke me . . .

Dog agrees enthusiastically.

(*Feeling his pockets.*) I can't find it.

Conductor Ticket, please, sir.

Kay I had it when we left Musborough . . .

Dog paws at Kay, whining.

It's no good, dog. Unless you know where my ticket is?

Dog scrapes at the floor, barking. Kay looks and picks up his ticket.

Kay You found it! Clever dog!

Conductor About time, lad.

Conductor punches his ticket and moves on, not impressed. The train goes into a tunnel . . .
And there is Cole Hawlings with his showman's trunk. He seems . . . familiar.

Cole I see my Barney dog has made a new friend. For this is the time that likings are made.

Kay He found my ticket! That was close.

Cole No doubt it slipped out while you rumpaged.

Kay I must have fallen asleep. He saved Christmas all right. I don't know how to thank you.

Cole Perhaps one day I shall ask you to do the same.

Kay Do what?

Cole Save Christmas. Young Master Harker, save Christmas when the wolves are running!

Darkness as the train enters another tunnel. Is that a train whistle or a wolf howl?

When they emerge, Cole and Barney have vanished. Instead: Charles, in a clerical dog collar, and his mate Joe, in a priest's hat.

Charles Going home for the Christmas holidays, ha-ha, what?

Kay Yes, from school, but –

Joe Just the weather for it, too. Snow! I like snow. Do you like snow, Kay Harker?

Kay Wait. How do you know my name?

Joe Are you travelling far, my young knight?

Charles This is wild country.

Joe In such deep snow.

Charles Some say pagan country.

Kay Just to . . . Condicote.

Joe And then to Seekings House –

Charles By any chance, ha-ha, what?

Kay Yes, but how did you –

Joe – Charles here and I are visiting the Missionary College.

Charles At Hope-under-Chesters.

Kay looks blank.

Joe You know! The old monastery, by the lake.

Charles (*crossing himself*) Such a grave and holy place.

Joe Alas, we will never be as pious and good as the great Abner Brown –

Charles – Our most reverend master, ha-ha what!

Joe Here – seeing it's the holidays, how about a little card trick? Doesn't he have the face for card tricks, Charles?

Charles The very face, Joe, just the angle . . .

Kay I don't know . . .

Charles Well, you soon will! Now, my young friend (*Taps his nose.*) 'Follow the Lady.'

He shuffles a pack of cards.

Watch the whirling cards . . . they shift, they lift, they dive . . . and now?

He deals three face down.

Which one is she?

Kay (*pointing*) That one.

Charles Didn't I tell you, Joe, that he had a clever face?

Joe Such a clever little face.

Charles Clever enough to spy an old man and his dog, ha-ha what?

Joe An old man and a dog that are of very great interest to us. Did you see such a pair pass this way, brave knight?

Kay I'm . . . not sure exactly.

Charles (*moving on*) In that case, my young squire, shall we add some incentive? If you beat me again, you shall have a sixpence. But if I beat you, you shall give me –

Joe Half a crown.

Charles A deal, ha-ha what?

Kay gets out his wallet.

Kay This is all I have – it's my Christmas pocket money.

Joe You want to watch out. There are strangers on trains who could have their eye on that. You want to be careful.

Kay I am always very careful.

Charles shuffles and deals again.

Charles We shall see about that. There. Which one is the Lady?

Kay looks down, but the cards have all disappeared.

Hard luck, old fruit.

Kay They've gone! How did you do that?

Charles Magic, no doubt. Half a crown, please. It will aid the Retired Rats' Home at Condicote.

Joe (*holding out his hand*) A more deserving cause, I do not know.

Kay digs in his pocket for a coin.

Kay Retired Rats?

Joe They grow very infirm in their old age.

Kay hesitates. Joe snatches the coin while Charles lifts his wallet.

It's a terrible sight. Let us hope you are never subjected to it.

The train huffs to a halt.

Charles Ah – this is Condicote, is it not?

Joe Indeed it is. Our stop and Mr Harker's. (*Suddenly scheming.*) Where the hawks get out to wait for the chicken . . .

Kay Please, how do you –

But they've disappeared.

– know all about me?

Kay pats his pockets.

My wallet!

The train melts away into the merry chaos of a rural train station at Christmas.
   Condicote!
   Kay is ejected into a crowd of passengers with tottering piles of gift boxes, and carol singers.
   And waiting for him is Sylvia Daisy Pouncer, in a veil and fur stole.

Pouncer Kay Harker? Are you waiting for Caroline Louisa?

Kay Yes, but I can't see her anywhere.

Pouncer It's the oddest coincidence! I spied her in a queue for the butcher's like you wouldn't believe. I thought, poor Caroline Louisa. She'll be desperate with worry. Why don't I collect him?

Kay That's very kind of you . . . Mrs –

Pouncer I'll tell you what. My motor car is just over there. It's very powerful and fast. If you trot along and climb inside, I will explain everything. You see –

She snarls – and flees, as we see Cole and Barney magically appearing.

Cole (*bowing to Kay*) Young Master Harker.

Kay I thought you'd disappeared. People keep coming and going today! (*Patting Dog.*) Hello, Barney! . . .

Cole Cole Hawlings, at your service. Are you . . . waiting for someone?

Kay My guardian, Caroline Louisa. At least, I think so . . . How about you?

Cole I suppose you could call me a wandering showman, of sorts.

Kay (*pointing to the case*) Like . . . a Punch and Judy man?

Cole If you like. Let me show you something that will make it clearer.

Cole produces a small box which catches the light.

Kay That looks very old.

Cole Older than you know.

Kay What's inside?

Cole Secrets. Magic secrets – that must not be had by those who crave their power. I think you know who I mean.

Cole locks the box away again.

Kay Those two vicars! They were looking for you! And that woman who offered me a lift . . . was she with them too?

Cole I fear the wolves are running once more. Can you help me stop their bite?

Kay Wolves? I don't know . . .

Cole No other soul can do this for me but you alone, Kay Harker. Christmas itself depends upon it!

In the crowd, Caroline Louisa appears, flustered, calling for Kay.

Caroline Kay? Kay?

Kay (*to Cole*) That's my guardian. You must have mistaken me for someone else. I'm just a schoolboy. I should go.

Cole When wolves run, it is better to know than not, Master Harker. You shall find me at The Drop of Dew if they come again. Now go! Time and tide and buttered eggs wait for no man.

Caroline There you are! I thought I'd never find you.

Kay Caroline Louisa!

They hug tight, a genuine bond.

And this is –

But Cole and Barney have vanished.

Oh! Where did they go?

Caroline Who? Never mind. My darling Kay! I was worried I might have missed you.

Kay I would never miss Christmas!

Caroline I know. And what a holiday it will be. The thousandth Christmas at Tatchester Cathedral. Quite a thing!

Kay It nearly wasn't, though . . . I lost my ticket until a dog called Barney found it, and then just now, a vicar showed me a card trick, and someone stole my wallet.

Caroline A vicar? Doing a card trick? Well, I never. First, the Post Office changed its opening hours, and now this. Condicote is just one surprise after another these days, I can't keep up . . . truly.

Kay He was strange, and his friend was even stranger. They knew my name . . . and my address at Seekings.

Caroline They could have spied that on your luggage labels. Did you notice any other suspicious people?

Kay Only this woman . . . There was something odd about her. And she offered me a lift in her motor car.

Caroline That's not suspicious, Kay; this is Condicote, not New York! Now come along; we mustn't be late – it's buttered eggs for tea.

Kay Buttered eggs! Mr Hawlings... He knew that too!

Caroline Who knew what?

Kay Mr Hawlings – the Punch and Judy man!

Caroline Well, let's worry no more about it. Now, there's something else I should tell you. It might be rather a shock, I'm afraid. We have the Jones children staying with us as well this year.

Kay Maria?

Caroline Yes, with her brother Peter – their father has been posted to India.

Kay I do hope Maria has brought some pistols. She normally has one or two.

Caroline I hope she has brought nothing of the kind. Now *come along*!

Kay drags his case off after Caroline as the carol singers sing, Condicote Station melting away into the cosy parlour of Seekings as they do.

Carol Singers
Hark how the bells,
Sweet silver bells,
all seem to say,
throw cares away

Christmas is here,
bringing good cheer,
to young and old,
meek and the bold.

Gaily they ring
while people sing
songs of good cheer,
Christmas is here!

SCENE THREE: GUNS FOR CHRISTMAS

Seekings House, a happy sprawl of rugs, armchairs and lamps and an oil painting of a wintry landscape.
Teatime. Kay is reunited with Maria Jones, thirteen, going on twenty-five, and her brother Peter, twelve, going on fifty.

Maria A Punch and Judy man? *A Punch and Judy man?* It's been over a year since I've seen you, Kay Harker, and you're still a total ass. Why didn't you ask him to do his show here?

Kay He said I had to stop some wolves, as Christmas depends on it. What do you think he meant?

Maria That modern advertising leaves a great deal to be desired . . . He was trying to get you to book him for his show, don't you see?

Peter I can't say that Caroline Louisa would approve, Maria.

Maria Oh, Peter! If you weren't my brother, I would pop an orange in your mouth every time you opened it; you marvellous bore.

Peter I wish you would be civil to me for once.

Maria I wish we would hear about a gang of jewel thieves in the neighbourhood who have come down to rob us while we are having our Christmas lunch! But we are ready and waiting for them – and there is the most glorious gunfight!

Peter I don't want guns for Christmas. I want plum pudding and a posset before bed.

Maria I only want a posset if there is a lot of brandy in it, or at the very least, sherry.

The others look at her in amazement.

What? Christmas ought to be brought up to date. It ought to have gangsters, aeroplanes and a *lot* of machine guns.

She points a toy gun at Kay.

(*Gangster accent.*) 'Your money or your life!'

Kay (*hands in the air, only half playing*) I told you! I've lost all my money.

Maria jabs the gun at his chest.

Will you settle for a Punch and Judy show?

Maria If you can find the old man. But be quick!

Kay I'd better ask Caroline Louisa first –

Maria aims the gun again.

All right! I'll walk into town. He said he would be at The Drop of Dew.

Maria No doubt the roughest inn in town! The kind full of cut-throats and smugglers. That's where his sort hangs out.

Peter Are you sure you want to go out in this weather? Look. It's started to snow.

So it has.

Kay (*wistful*) Perhaps there will be enough to make a snowman tomorrow.

Peter I don't like building snowmen. Your hands get frostbite, and they always melt in the end.

Maria You are too dull for Christmas! The sentence is death!

Maria chases Peter off to bed with her gun.
 Kay grabs his overcoat just as Caroline Louisa enters with a lamp.

Caroline Kay! Where are you going?

Kay I thought I might walk down to Condicote.

Caroline At this time of day? Whatever for?

Kay To go . . . (*Improvises.*) to the baker for some muffins! If we're having buttered eggs.

Caroline You are such a darling. Very well – in that case, while you're there, you might ask the baker for an extra plum pudding . . . And don't be long! I want us to sit down together for tea . . .

He's gone.

. . . like we're a real family.

Caroline Louisa is alone, and as Seekings melts away, she looks out at the falling snow and, as Kay makes his way to Condicote, she sings:

In the bleak midwinter
Frosty wind made moan,
Earth stood hard as iron,
Water like a stone;
Snow had fallen, snow on snow,
Snow on snow,
In the bleak midwinter
Long ago.

SCENE FOUR: A PHOENIX

Kay crosses Condicote Market as the snow falls, and the day darkens. Even the stalls of turkeys, fruit and cakes, etc., look threatening.

Butcher Turkeys! Geese! Suckling pig!

Kay Excuse me, do you know where –

Grocer Oranges! Apples! Sweets!

Kay I'm looking for The Drop of Dew –

Baker Christmas cake! Mince Pies! Plum pudding!

Kay Oh – one plum pudding, please, and some muffins, too.

He hands her some coins. Baker gives him a bag of muffins with change.

Baker There you are, Master Kay.

Kay Do you know . . . where The Drop of Dew is?

But as he looks up from pocketing his change – they've gone, except for one woman, shrouded in a shawl.

Hello? Miss? Excuse me –

Her shawl falls. All we can see are piercing, shining eyes. Her voice echoes.

Herne The wolves are running! If you see someone, say someone's safe.

Kay Someone? Who?

We hear wolves draw near. Just in time, Kay reaches The Drop of Dew Inn. Cole sits in a corner, with Barney at his feet.

Kay (*slowly approaching Cole*) If I saw someone, I was to tell someone that someone was safe.

Cole Ah, but that's more than anyone knows when wolves run.

Kay Please, sir, what do you mean by 'wolves'?

Cole When wolves are abroad, they take many forms.

Kay Mr Hawlings, my friends, they asked me –

Cole – would I go to Seekings with my Punch and Judy show?

Kay How do you keep knowing what I'm going to say?

Cole It is of no matter. But I will be there.

Kay That will make their Christmas! Are you . . . very expensive, though?

Cole How if I was to say a biscuit for Barney and a dish of eggs and bacon for me?

Kay I'm sure we can manage that!

Cole Now, as you have rumpaged all the way here, I'll show you what those wolves are after.

Cole sets the Box on the table.

It is my Box of Delights.

Kay Sorry, we haven't done that at school yet.

Cole It is not taught in schools, nor will it ever be.

Beat.

But first, tell me what you would most like to see in the world.

Kay I would like to see my mother and father again, more than anything.

Cole Why? When did you last see them?

Kay A long time ago . . . six years this Christmas . . . there was a fire.

Cole Master Kay. This Box is full of old magic. It carries the weight of ages past and burns with the desire of those seeking to possess its delights. It can do many things. But it cannot bring back the dead into the land of the living.

Kay's silence speaks for itself.

(*Kindly.*) Perhaps then – is there anything that might remind you of them?

Kay I'm not sure . . . yes . . . there was a brooch my mother always wore. It was destroyed in the fire. A golden phoenix. But phoenixes don't exist, either, do they?

Cole Ah, perhaps they do.

Cole opens the Box, and their faces light up.

Look at the desert sands, where the pebbles are diamonds . . . Look now, the spice tree. Can you smell it?

The Box makes a glittering phoenix appear.

Kay A phoenix! My mother once told me they could sing. Do you think this one can?

Phoenix sings, a haunting cry.

Cole Listen.

The magical bird disappears –

Kay No, it's gone!

Cole Keep watching, Still watch

– then is reborn in a ball of fire before flying off.

Kay (*subdued*) It was just a trick, though.

Cole Master Kay, there are tricks, what court jesters are known for, and then there is magic . . . which can change the fate of the earth we stand upon. Magic of space and time. One is much harder and rarer than the other, so we must always beware of those doing only tricks.

Kay Like those vicars on the train, the ones from the Missionary College . . .

Cole But come along now, the snow is deepening . . .

The snow begins again –

So you shall see me at Seekings, with my Punch and Judy and my little dog Barney at one half after five . . . So, for now, Mr Harker – Barney!

Cole collects his Box and Barney before disappearing into the snow.

SCENE FIVE: A KIND OF PUNCH AND JUDY SHOW

Seekings.
Ellen is serving a tea of toasted muffins to Maria, Peter and Kay by the fire.

Peter Well done, Kay. You wouldn't catch me out in the snow on a wild goose chase after some strange old man you met on a train.

Ellen takes away the tea things, leaving the children alone.

Kay It was odd. No one else seems to have seen Mr Hawlings. I wonder if he was just in a dream. It's as if I made him up.

Peter Do you do that a lot?

Kay What?

Peter Make things up.

Kay People at school say I do.

Peter I wish I could make things up.

Maria Poor Peter doesn't even know how to make a joke.

Peter Listen, Kay, you don't seriously think this Punch and Judy man is a magician, do you?

The French windows blow open with a bang in a gust of snow! There is Cole, with his case and Barney.

Kay Mr Hawlings! And Barney too.

Peter immediately befriends Barney.

Cole It is a wild night, Master Harker, as wild as any I've known – and I've been a long time on the roads.

Maria (*suspicious*) How long?

Cole Well, first, there were pagan times. Then there were in-between times, then Christian times, then the pudding times. But the times I liked best were the in-between times.

Maria Well, you might also know this time as teatime – (*Jabs toasting fork at him.*) and I, for one, am jolly hungry for our show!

Peter I am so sorry about my sister, sir. She is quite the rudest member of my entire family. Can I offer you a buttered muffin?

Cole Don't you worry, Master Peter. Perhaps a sausage for Barney here. Now . . .

The puppet theatre becomes a magical show, as much magic lantern as puppets.

Once, long ago, there was a great wizard, and his name was Ramon Lully.

Ramon appears, a wise old elder with a tiny puppet dog.

Ramon was famous throughout the land for his magical gifts. Yet he had a rival.

Arnold appears, sharp and sly, with a waxed moustache.

Arnold of Todi. An evil sorcerer so powerful that no one dared say who was the greatest, him or Ramon. There was only one way to decide.

Peter A parliamentary enquiry!

Maria A knife fight to the death!

Cole They made a wager. To see who could come up with a piece of magic so incredible that it had never been done before.

Peter I'd like to see the trains run on time at Christmas. That has never been done before.

Maria I'd like to see a tale about a woman told by a woman.

Kay Shh!

Ramon and Arnold shake hands and disappear.

Cole Ramon and Arnold went away for a year and a day.

The seasons pass in the puppet show.

Then, at Christmas, Ramon reappeared with a vial of oil he had found in the desert. An elixir – anyone who drank it would live for all eternity!

Ramon returns, brandishing a vial that sparkles brightly.

Peter What's an elixir?

Maria Keep up, Peter. Like cough medicine, but you live forever.

Cole But then, Arnold of Todi returned with a magic box of his own creation. A box of many delights, the greatest of which was the ability to travel through time.

Arnold reappears with a glowing box . . .

Kay The Box of Delights!

He disappears and then reappears . . . with medieval knights in armour on horseback . . . then disappears and reappears on a pirate ship, and finally . . . in 1930s London with buses and taxis . . .

Peter Time travel gives me a headache.

Maria So go on then – who won?

Cole There was no winner, Miss Maria. The very next day, Arnold of Todi disappeared, taking his Box with him. And he has never been seen since until . . .

He is interrupted by a wolf howling ominously. Barney barks in response.

Peter Someone must have let their dog out.

Kay That isn't a dog, Peter; it's a wolf.

Maria Nobody move! I'm going to fetch my pirate costume. That will scare off any wolf.

Cole It is the snow that brings the wolves out. Many a bitter night did we see them off before, but now, once more, they're running in many forms. We must stand by our spears.

Maria Spears! That is the best idea anyone has had all day. There are curtain poles in our bedroom – come on, Peter, let's make ourselves a spear or two!

Maria drags Peter off.
  We sense a pack of wolves drawing in. Barney growls, and lights flicker.

Cole The pack has surrounded us, as wolves are wont to do. They've run me close this time.

Kay Why do they want you so badly?

Cole My Box of Delights. That which I showed you at The Drop of Dew.

The windows shake violently; something powerful is trying to get in.
  Barney suddenly growls like a much bigger dog – holding it off briefly.
  Cole produces the Box of Delights.

If I hand that to you, Master Harker, will you keep it safe for me? Christmas depends upon it.

Kay Shouldn't you go to the police?

Cole shakes his head. The wolves whine for the Box.

Cole The police cannot stop these wolves. For this Box does not belong to me. It belongs to –

Kay Arnold of Todi! The evil sorcerer in your play. (*Realises.*) You stole it!

Cole He could have done so much good with this Box; instead, all he wants is harm. This Box is full of old magic. You must handle it with great care.

Kay Why? What can it do?

Cole It can do three things.

He gives Kay the Box, which glows and shudders with a magical hum.

Cole Here's the first. Do you see this lever? If you push it to the right, you can go as small as a mouse. Second, if you press it to the left, you can go as swift as a falcon.

Kay What's the third thing?

Cole The third . . . is the most powerful delight of the Box, but also the most dangerous.

A clawed paw pushes through a door. Cole points to the painting from the attic scene – now hanging on display.

Quick. Tell me – what is that picture there?

Kay It's of Bottler's Down, a wood just outside Condicote.

Cole A picture you love and know well?

Kay My father painted it. It was the only one of his that survived the fire.

Cole And now you look it at afresh, with your young eyes, do you perhaps see something new?

The painting shimmers, a fuse blows and a brief powercut blackout. Cole and Barney vanish.

(*Voice-over.*) Look after the Box, Master Harker! Guard it with your life. To save Christmas!

They are now part of the picture as if they had been painted there all along.

Kay With my life? Mr Hawlings! Come back!

The French windows fly open. Charles and Joe, disguised as carol singers, enter.

Charles What ho, Master Harker! We meet again. Are we too late for the puppet show? Ha-ha what?

Kay (*coldly*) I think you'll find Mr Hawlings has already left.

He points to the door.

That way.

Joe What a shame. I love a nice show, I do. A bit of the old Punch.

Kay You stole my wallet on the train. I think you should go.

Joe You're getting a bit sharp for my liking, young knight.

Kay He's gone, and you won't find him.

Charles Oh, won't we? We'll have to see about that, ha-ha what . . .

They grab Kay just as Maria and Peter return. Maria is dressed as a terrifying pirate: a fiery beard and eye patch, armed to the teeth with knives. She pulls along Peter in an ill-fitting Smee costume on a leash.

Maria (*in pirate voice*) Aargh, landlubbers!

Joe That is quite a beard, little girl.

Maria I'm sorry, but we are playing pirates now, and you're not invited, so you have to leave. Goodbye.

Charles But –

Maria throws one of her knives into the door frame by his head. The intruders need little persuading as she shoos them out.

Peter Maria! You are so rude to guests. What will Caroline Louisa think? I didn't even have time to offer them a cup of tea.

Kay No, Peter, they weren't our guests. They were thieves. Or wolves . . . I think they want to do something bad to Mr Hawlings.

Maria (*yelling out of the door*) Come back! Come back! I challenge you to a cutlass duel! To the death!

The real Cathedral Choir – men and women in clerical garb with Japanese lanterns, arrive outside, singing 'First Noel'.

Choir
Noel, Noel, Noel, Noel
Born is the King of Israel!

They looked up and saw a star,
Shining in the East beyond them far
And to the earth it gave great light,
And so it continued both day and night.

Noel, Noel, Noel, Noel
Born is the King of Israel!
Born is the King of Israel!

Peter (*running to the window, speaking over singing*) Carol singers!

Maria How ghastly. Shall I rush upstairs and tip a cauldron of boiling oil over them?

Caroline enters with Ellen.

Caroline I'd rather if you didn't, Maria – it's the Tatchester Cathedral Choir, including the Bishop himself and the Mayor of Condicote! I need you to help Ellen hand around the hot chocolate. Quick march, please!

The Choir fills the study from all sides, in full voice. And when they part, we see –
 The children watching the Bishop and Mayor slowly drain their cocoa, surrounded by the choir.
 Caroline Louisa, a twitching model of politeness.

Bishop And now, dear lady, I fear we must conclude this happy tour and make our way back.

Caroline Ellen – can you ask the Bishop's driver to bring his car round, please?

Ellen Yes, I can.

Beat. She stands there.

Caroline Well then, will you?

Ellen flounces off. The Bishop makes to follow but then stops at the door.

Bishop Oh! I nearly forgot. Children! I must return your kind hospitality. Tomorrow night, the Mayor and I are hosting a Christmas party. Five o'clock at Tatchester Cathedral.

Mayor There are games, and the Duchess of Musborough will give out the prizes.

Bishop And best of all, the Reverend Abner Brown from the Missionary College has generously donated a Christmas tree. With electric lights and –

Caroline Is this part of the celebrations for the thousandth Christmas at Tatchester?

Bishop Just the beginning, Caroline Louisa, just the very beginning! There will be a special service on Christmas Eve, the first of its kind in the country –

Mayor Then there's going to be the carol concert in the town square, fireworks and a grand procession. Most magnificent! Folk are coming from everywhere – not just Condicote, but Newminster, Musborough . . . Yockwardine!

Caroline Yockwardine! Goodness, that does rather change things. I'd better buy a hat.

Bishop But we'll start with our tea party tomorrow, and you're all invited!

Peter Even Maria?

Bishop Yes, Peter, especially my friend little Maria.

Maria Even though last year, I started your car and drove it into a lamp post?

Bishop Christmas is a time for forgiveness, my dear . . . You will be most welcome at our party.

The Bishop and Mayor leave. Ellen returns with a telegram on a silver tray for Caroline.

Ellen This telegram just arrived for you, ma'am.

Caroline reads the telegram.

Kay Caroline Louisa! Those pickpockets disguised as vicars broke in looking for Mr Hawlings, but he escaped through a painting!

Caroline My dearest Kay – I can't take any of that in, I'm afraid. I've had awful news.

She stumbles. Kay steadies her.

Maria (*thrilled*) Are we at war?

Caroline No, Maria! It's my brother. He has suddenly been taken very ill. I have to take the last train up tonight to see him. I'm sorry.

Kay But that means –

Caroline Yes, Kay, I am afraid it means that I won't be here for the first night of the holidays.

Kay You're leaving us on our own.

Caroline I'll be back tomorrow . . . or as soon as I can. I'm sure you'll manage. And Ellen will look after you. (*To Ellen.*) Can you tell Cook I won't be here for supper?

Ellen Yes, I can.

Beat. She stands there.

Caroline Well then, will you?

Ellen flounces out.

So be good, children, I'll be home for Christmas.

She sees their faces.

I promise!

Caroline kisses Kay and leaves. For a moment, the children are disconcerted and abandoned.

Kay Alone at Christmas. Again.

Maria You're not alone, Kay, though, are you?

Peter (*finally*) Well. Now everyone's gone, can I go up the stairs to Bedfordshire early with my book? It's on naval history.

Maria Don't you see? We can have a proper adventure now! One with real blood. Shall we rough up some vicars?

Kay No . . . If the wolves are after us, then I shall be like a wolf too . . . and track their footprints.

Kay puts his coat on and steps through the windows.

Maria This is going to be the best Christmas ever!

Beat.

Oh, and Kay?

Kay Yes, Maria?

Maria Try not to get eaten by any wolves, won't you?

Kay I'll try!

Maria drags Peter away as Kay sets off through the snow, following Charles and Joe's footprints, as Seekings disappears and he finds –

SCENE SIX: ABNER BROWN

The Missionary College – a spooky, ivy-clad Gothic monastery. An eerie silence apart from an owl hooting. Kay takes the Box out.

Kay (*whispers*) What did Mr Hawlings say? Press to the right to go –

He shrinks to Tiny Kay –

– Oh! As small as a mouse! It works!

Charles and Joe approach through the old cloisters, flashing their torches.

The sound of wolves from all sides, approaching stealthily. Charles and Joe search anxiously with their torches. Abner, a devil in a silk dressing gown, pops up behind them.

Abner You missed the old man – for the second time.

Joe You'd have thought him . . . one of them carol singers, chief . . . just as we did.

Abner Would I, gentle Joe, my far-seeing friend? I wonder. You have heard my wolves are a-running. Would you like them to run for you?

The wolves growl, panting, drawing nearer.

Joe No, chief.

Abner Charles! I was told you were the best at scrobbling in London. You cost a fair penny. Well? My wolves are waiting. They are hungry tonight.

Charles It's . . . as Joe said. He must have escaped . . . disguised as one of the carol singers.

Abner Cole Hawlings. One of the greatest magicians of space and time . . . escaped disguised as a provincial carol singer?

Charles He had a, er, very convincing costume. And a marvellous singing voice . . . a deep bass . . . (*He demonstrates.*) 'Good King Wenceslas looked out on the feast of . . .'

He loses his nerve.

Abner 'Stephen'?

Charles 'Stephen'.

Deathly pause.

Abner My dear, soft lads, did you know that I am also a magician?

They did.
He pulls on a sinister diamond-studded leather glove.

I, too, can make people sing. Not just people. Children. Pets. Do you want to see how?

They don't.
Abner points his gloved hand at both Charles and Joe, who choke for breath, jerking around.

Do you hear that sweet music, Pouncer, my Queen of the Night? Pouncer!

With a flick of his hand, he summons Pouncer from the shadows. Kay gasps.

Pouncer My Lord of Darkness, my Abner Brown. I am here at your command.

Abner Well? Or do you believe he was singing carols too?

Pouncer He is a clever wretch – who no doubt used the old magic to outwit your wolves in a way that not even you could have foreseen, Omniscient One.

Abner (*to Charles and Joe*) Hawlings escaped you on the train, and now he has again. I am losing my patience, and trust me: you do not want to see me lose my patience.

He releases them, and they fall to the ground, spent.

Where is my Rat? Perhaps he can tell me something useful. Rat!

We hear echoing, squeaking beneath us.

Where are you? Curse your rotten tail!

He drags Rat from his hiding place: a greasy, piratical rodent.

Rat Down in the cellars and tunnels I run, all weathers, all hours – for one 'oo would sell 'is own mother, if 'e 'ad one, to be ground down into old bones.

Abner You are too kind. Now tell me what you know, Rat, before I grind you into old bones.

Rat Maybes I will, maybes I won't. 'Oo's the lovely lady, Abner?

Abner This, Rat, is my new partner in crime – Sylvia Daisy Pouncer, and you will do well to watch your words with her.

Rat Why, is she a witch?

Pouncer (*smiling sweetly*) Like you wouldn't believe. Give us your news, unless you want to meet my black cat. He has rather a fondness for rats. Especially their eyes.

Rat Wot will I get for it? I could kill for a piece of green cheese.

Pouncer Here is some green cheese for you, then.

She produces something so revolting that even Charles and Joe are shocked.

What do you know about Hawlings and his Box?

Abner My Box!

Rat You will find 'im you seek at the place they call Bottler's Down.

Charles Bottler's Down? Impossible! He went to Tatchester with the Bishop and the choir.

Joe We saw him, guv, with our own eyes.

Rat You asked me wot I know; this is wot I know. I 'eard it through the wainscoting. 'Ee used magic to escape through a painting before you even opened the door! (*To Pouncer.*) 'Ave you any more of that cheese? Just a little crumb? Please?

Pouncer And will he have the . . . goods on him?

Rat Ooh, wot a clever question. So I'll ask again, do you 'ave more of that cheese? I need it. My cheese! Please. Cheese!

Abner Silence, you repulsive rodent! I need that Box by Christmas Eve. The thousandth Christmas at Tatchester Cathedral.

Rat For some bacon rind? Go on, guv, just one little scrap of bacon rind. It makes my fur shine so, and that's the truth. Go on.

Abner Very well! For bacon rind! Just tell me how to get my Box!

Pouncer gives Rat his bacon.

Rat If you want that Box, you must scrobble 'im at Bottler's Down tomorrow at dawn.

Abner Charles, Joe, do you think you can follow a simple instruction this time?

Charles Scrobbling old men in the snow? I was hoping for a little more glamour.

Abner I won't ask you again. Or do you want a visit to . . . the Scrounger?

A tiny sneak preview of the Scrounger: hiss of smoke and faintest mechanical roar.

Joe No fear!

Abner Then how many times do I need to tell you? Get to Bottler's Down! Get!

Charles and Joe hurry off.

Rat One last fing, though, I swear . . . in the tavern and at this 'ouse, the old man – 'ee was talking to this little lad –

Abner Don't say the name –

Rat – Harker! I only says wot I see!

Abner Get back down that hole before I throw you there.

Rat disappears with a giant splash.

Abner We can brook no interference from a meddling child.

Pouncer Have no fear, my darkness. That dreamy little muff is no threat to us.

Abner Let us hope you are right. Our plans are too advanced now to fail.

They disappear into the shadows.
   A tumble of stones as a watcher appears from his hiding place. Tiny Kay.

Tiny Kay That's what you think . . . Abner Brown.

He produces the Box and transforms himself back into Kay.

Now let's see if the other lever does as the old man promised . . . Box . . . go swift . . . straight to Seekings!

The Box shakes and glows before rising into the air, taking Kay with it.
   A moment of wonder, and then he cries out as he vanishes into the darkness.

SCENE SEVEN: BOTTLER'S DOWN

Kay reappears with a flash outside Seekings – to find Maria and Peter in their coats, waiting for him. It's snowing.

Peter Where have you been? Maria has been torturing me all evening.

Maria We thought a gang had abducted you.

Peter You've got gangs on the brain, Maria.

Kay Those thieves are in a gang, all right. And their leader is a strange devil in a silk dressing gown called Abner Brown, who has sent his wolves to scrobble Mr Hawlings at Bottler's Down. We have to stop them. Will you come with me?

Maria I'd rather do anything than go to bed.

Peter But to be out in the middle of the night on the first day of the holidays – I think it's the Purple Pim, I truly do.

Maria Don't worry, Peter; I foraged in the larder. Look.

She shows him what her pockets are stuffed with.

Peter Mince pies! Then what are we waiting for?

The children set off into the night. A blizzard whips around them, but they eventually find a space to wait. And wait . . . And watch . . .

Peter (*shivering*) People say snow can be warm if you get into it.

Maria Yes, that's just the kind of thing people say.

Peter I heard it at school, so it must be true.

Maria 'I heard it at school, so it must be true.' I wish you would trust more in the school of life instead of some nonsense a teacher told you.

Peter I wish Papa and Mama were here so they could stop your nonsense!

Beat.

Kay, do you miss your mother and father at Christmas?

Kay I do, Peter. Every year. More than you can imagine.

Peter Look – I can see something.

He points.

Maria It's the Punch and Judy man with his dog!

We see Cole struggling through the snow with Barney . . . as a car driven by Charles and Pouncer appears behind him.

Kay (*yelling*) Mr Hawlings! Mr Hawlings!

Cole can't hear over the storm. Rat leaps up from behind some snow and throws a net over him.

Maria They're scrobbling him!

Kay Stop them!

The children run over, screaming for 'Mr Hawlings!' as he is bundled into the car.

Peter Too late!

Maria Ha! They'll never get away in this snow. Come on.

Kay Wait –

They start back as the car revs up, and then all we can see are the dazzling headlights.
  The wings extend – and it swoops up into the air over their heads!
  Then they are alone again in the snow.

Peter I say, Kay, I am glad I came out with you. I never thought I should see a rat abduct a Punch and Judy man by putting a bag over his head and carrying him off in a car that turned into an aeroplane.

Maria Where next? I can smell adventure!

Kay Look. There's something I have to tell you both. Before Mr Hawlings left Seekings, he gave me this box. I have to keep it safe for him; I promised on my life. It's the most special thing I've ever been given.

Kay produces the Box of Delights with a flourish.

Maria What's inside?

Kay That's just it . . . I don't know. Do you remember the play about the two wizards? Ramon Lully's Elixir of Life –

Maria (*excited*) And Arnold of Todi's Box of Delights!

Kay Exactly. And I think this is it.

Maria Well, go on then? What does it do, Mr Todi's precious Box?

Kay He said that if I pushed the lever to the right, I would go small – and I do! Then, if I moved it to the left, I would go swift. And I do!

Maria Never mind the lever . . . what's inside?

Kay He didn't say.

Maria Kay Harker. What is the point of having a Box of Delights if we can't delight in it? Open the box!

Kay Very well.

As he does, the Box sparkles. An intense sound of birdsong surrounds them.
The Box opens slowly, light filling their faces – Herne the Hunter, an antler-horned and caped goddess, rises magnificently out of the dark.
Her eyes shine in a way we have seen before.

Kay It's you! The lady from the market.

Herne Hello again, Kay. Hello children.

Maria My parents told me never to talk to strangers. Especially ones dressed like that. Who are you?

Herne I am Herne the Hunter, the Lady of the Oak. This box is made from my tree, and I remain its guardian. Welcome to my wild wood.

Herne Why don't you come in and take a closer look?

A magical forest of greenery and colour erupts from the surrounding snow.

Kay This is so beautiful! I shall never know even a hundredth of all the things there are to know!

Herne You will do if you stay with me. Become a stag and discover for yourself . . .

Kay is transformed into a stag that runs and jumps.

Kay It's so lovely to feel the grass beneath my feet!

Maria What do I get? In my opinion, the great failing of English woods is their lack of tigers.

Herne I think for you, Miss Maria . . . how about a wild duck?

Maria If you must . . . as long as I don't have to go anywhere near the water . . . ooh!

Maria sprouts wings and soars above our heads as a duck, honking.

Everything looks so little and far away . . . this is too much fun!

Peter (*depressed*) I suppose I have to become an animal, too, don't I?

Herne Yes, you do, Peter. To see the world through new eyes.

Peter And what have you chosen for me? A daring eagle, perhaps? Or a cunning fox?

Herne No, Peter. Not an eagle or a fox. A trout.

Peter becomes a trout, swimming through water and reeds.

Peter But how beautiful and fresh the water is!

The children thrill to their new sense of being.

Kay I could be a deer forever!

Maria And I a duck!

Peter Not entirely sure about this trout business.

Herne Be careful though, children . . . I told you the wood was wild.

The fantasy forest sky darkens.

Maria The wilder the better!

Herne Look out for the hawks in the sky, Maria.

Maria shrieks as a sharp-beaked hawk dives after her.

Peter Ha! A hawk can't catch me!

Herne Beware the pike in the reeds, Peter!

A massive scary pike closes in on Peter.

Kay What is this? What's going on?

Herne Watch out for the wolves in the woods, Kay!

Wolves with glowing red eyes appear in the shadows.

They have taken Cole; they will take others, but don't lose courage. You will beat the wolves, won't you, Kay?

Kay snaps the Box shut. Herne's wild wood vanishes. The children and the Box vanish swiftly.

SCENE EIGHT: UNFIT FOR LIFE

The dank vaults of the Missionary College. Water drips loudly. A large iron sluice wheel sticks up from the floor.
Pouncer enters warily.
She gets out her gun, just in case.
With a wolf growl, Abner appears directly behind, making her start.

Abner Pouncer . . . my queen. Are you all right? You look pale. The air under this lake is very foul.

Pouncer Not as foul as your breath.

Abner Thank you, my emerald. Have those fools done what I ordered or not?

Pouncer Rat! Reveal yourself, rodent!

Rat pops up, chewing and twitching.

(*Holding her nose.*) What have you got for us?

Rat Wot 'ave you got for mee . . . I needs it!

Pouncer Now what?

Rat I can't stand the climate like I used to . . . I know it's poison, but . . .

Pouncer Very well. One tot of rum for you, Rat.

She produces a hip-flask and pours Rat a thimble of rum.

Rat (*downing it*) 'Appy days! Ooh . . . I love a nice bit of poison I do!

Pouncer So, Rat, I ask you again. What did you get for us?

Rat chucks away the thimble and unlocks a door: Cole chained up behind bars.

Rat This is the bloke wot we scrobbled for yer. Then we tortured 'im.

Abner That's what I asked you to do, wretched vermin. So, what have you got for me?

Rat splutters.

Abner Speak up!

Rat Was I meant to do anything else?

Abner Oh, nothing much . . . maybe get me a fur hat for Pouncer here, a plum pudding for Cole and me to share . . . and my *Box*! The Box I sent you to get.

Rat We searched 'im from the top of 'is head to the bottom of 'is boots, but no Box fing did we find! See for yerself, if yer want . . .

Abner Useless vermin! I shall hang you by your tail till your eyes fall out of your skull!

Rat squeaks with fear. Abner turns to his prisoner and puts on his glove.

Master Hawlings. We meet again. You are in my power. It's quite simple. Tell where that Box is, my Box – and you live.

Cole Or?

Abner Or . . .

He points the glove at Cole – with no effect.

Cole Your cheap dark tricks will not work on me, rascal.

Shows a glittering vial around his neck.

I am still protected by my Elixir of Life, which will never be yours!

Abner lunges for the vial, but recoils, as if he's had an electric shock. It's clear he can't touch this magic, even with his glove.

Abner See this iron wheel? It works sluices by which I can flood these cellars at will.

He gives it a half-turn, a creak, a gurgle of water.

Now, what say you to that, old man?

Cole I say you are a villain, unfit for life!

Abner slams his cell door shut.

Abner Enough, you doddery fool! Rat . . . you swore this old man would give me my Box. You promised me.

Rat I only told you wot I saw!

Pouncer Too late to cry over spilt milk, my darkness.

Abner But not too late to make the spiller cry, my empress.

Abner aims his magic glove of doom.

You must have learned something from this old fool. Tell me!

Rat Begging your mercy, but maybe 'e gave it to the boy – Kay Harker?

Abner I'm sorry, did you say something?

Rat Yes –

Abner points his gloved hand at Rat, who chokes, but this time to death.

Abner I didn't think so. (*To Pouncer.*) There is not a moment to lose. We must bring forward the second part of our plan. You boasted you hired the best jewel thieves in London. Now is your chance to prove it. Take Charles and Joe. Search Seekings. Churn up Condicote and turn over Tatchester.

Pouncer Including the Cathedral?

Abner Especially the Cathedral. Scrobble who you have to. Steal what you must, but get me my Box!

Pouncer Might there be some truth in what that useless creature said? Perhaps Hawlings may have entrusted your precious box to a child?

Abner Who? Do I see a plan forming, my priceless pearl?

Pouncer A plan of perfection, my dear Abby!

SCENE NINE: THE BISHOP'S PARTY

Choir
  Deck the halls with boughs of holly
  Tra la la la la la la laaaaa
  Deck the halls with boughs of holly
  Tra la la la la la la la la
  'Tis the season to be jolly
  Tra la la la la la la la
  Fill the mead cup drain the barrel
  Fa la la la la la la la la
  Troll the ancient Christmas carol
  Fa la la la la lala la
  Strike the harp and join the chorus

Tra la la la la la la la la
'Tis the season to be jolly
Tra la la la la la la la!

Tatchester Cathedral, decorated gaily with paper chains, etc., for the Bishop's Party. A splendid Christmas tree piled around with presents. Tables and chairs.

And Maria. She disassembles her pistol on the handkerchief, then reassembles it . . . She checks her watch and starts over.

Pouncer enters behind her, in disguise.

Pouncer Miss Maria Jones?

Maria Who wants to know?

Pouncer What have you got there?

Maria (*distracted*) I'm seeing how fast I can take apart and reassemble my pistol.

She sees Pouncer's reaction.

It's the Bishop's Christmas party – I need to be prepared.

Pouncer This brings me to my reason for seeking you out.

Maria Well, spit it out.

She checks her watch again.

Pouncer I come with a message from the Bishop himself.

Maria points her pistol at Pouncer.

Not *that* kind of message. He heard you were rather keen on stained glass. Tatchester Cathedral is famous for it. And being an enthusiast himself, he wondered whether you might like to join him on a special tour of the windows in the Lady Chapel before the party begins.

Maria It's rather mouldy, the glass in the Lady Chapel.

Pouncer (*changing tack*) Miss Maria. We have more in common than it may appear. I, too, do not share the Bishop's enthusiasm for the glass in the Lady Chapel. And, like you, I never leave the house without my gun.

Maria Phooey! You dress like a dowager and talk like a nanny. I don't believe you're carrying so much as a sharpened knitting needle.

Pouncer I hate to disappoint one of such tender years, but I am neither a dowager nor a nanny. And this is very much a gun.

Pouncer produces a large pearl-handled revolver from her bag.

I ripped it from the cold, dead hands of a gangster when I was last in Chicago.

Maria Splendiferous!

Pouncer Aren't you shocked?

Maria No, I'm wondering why you kept that hidden under your lace handkerchief while you prattled on about stained glass?

Pouncer Do you like it then, Miss Maria?

Maria I want to fire it immediately. How many ruffians have you shot?

Pouncer I'm afraid I lost count after a hundred.

Maria Better and better! Please, may I see?

Pouncer (*holding gun back*) It's rather a large gun for such a little girl.

Maria I think you'll find it's what I do with it that counts.

Pouncer In that case, what do you say to a little competition?

Maria I only like to enter competitions in which I am guaranteed to win.

Pouncer Well, we shall see. I challenge you to reassemble your weapon quicker than I can mine.

Maria Easy. What are the terms?

Pouncer If you win, I shall leave you in peace. If I win, you must come with me to the Lady Chapel.

Maria Go on then. On the count of three. One. Two. Three.

Pouncer sets her watch, and they race to reassemble their guns. Maria wins by a whisker.

Maria Bad luck! Although that was fast for someone of your advanced years. Where did you learn to do that?

Pouncer I was raised by nuns. They were very keen on self-defence.

Maria As am I.

She points her gun at Pouncer.

And now I think you promised to leave me in peace.

Pouncer How you must enjoy the quiet atmosphere of school.

Maria School! I've been expelled from three, and their headmistresses still swoon when they hear my name. You see, I'm Maria Jones!

Pouncer Indeed you are, my dove, and – (*Removing her disguise.*) I am Sylvia Daisy Pouncer.

She scrobbles her off, just as the party guests whirl in – including Kay and Peter. The Bishop enters with the Mayor and tries to get his guests' attention by first coughing . . . then tinging a sherry glass . . . then clapping . . . Finally, the Mayor passes him a gong, which he sounds to terrifying effect.

Bishop My lords, ladies and gentlemen, boys and girls, welcome!

Mayor Where you now stand, pilgrims have stood for generations.

Bishop And tomorrow, at our midnight service on Christmas Eve, we will celebrate a thousand years of Christmas here at Tatchester Cathedral.

Mayor It will be the thousandth celebration since the Cathedral was founded.

Everyone cheers!

We want this to be the most special and spectacular Christmas ever! We're very honoured to be joined by her grace, the Duchess of Musborough, who will hand out the prizes for our party games later.

The Duchess appears, glittering with diamonds, and gives a regal wave.

Bishop So, let us make merry. And we'll begin – with some presents!

The guests swarm over the pile of gifts, apart from Peter and Kay.

Peter This is what Christmas is all about, Kay!

The Bishop approaches them with the Mayor.

Bishop Hello Peter, hello Kay. Wonderful that you're both here. I have something to give you. Mayor? Would you be so kind?

Mayor hands Peter a scarlet and white stocking from the gift pile.

Peter (*pulls out a toy sleigh*) A sleigh . . . and even better, it's full of chocolate creams!

Bishop Kay . . .

He hands Kay a gift.

I know this time of year is always difficult for you . . . We thought you might enjoy this wonder.

The party fades as Kay unwraps his present. He holds it up, marvelling – a beautiful toy ship, tall sails gleaming – joy.

Kay (*reading inscription in awe*) 'Captain Kidd's Fancy'!

Peter (*downcast*) Chocolate creams.

The Mayor hands the Bishop an outsized parcel shaped like a machine gun.

Bishop And . . . I got this for my young friend Maria, to show there were no hard feelings after last year's mishap . . . Oh! Is she not with you?

Peter We thought she was playing next door.

Bishop I'm afraid I haven't seen her at all.

Kay But she took a bus here earlier . . .

Bishop Not to worry, I'm sure she'll turn up.

Peter That's so unlike her to miss a party! Your Grace . . . Please, may I use your telephone to call Seekings and check she is all right?

Bishop Of course, Peter, you must . . . the Mayor will show you where to go.

Peter leaves with the Mayor, as Charles whirls past, dressed as a vicar again, dancing with the Duchess and lifting her necklace during the following exchange, to Kay's horror.

Bishop Ah, good evening, Brother Charles! All going splendidly at the Missionary College, I trust?

Charles Sparkling, Your Grace! Ha-ha what?

Bishop Delighted you could make it.

The Mayor returns, out of sorts.

Mayor It's a disaster!

The music and party abruptly come to a halt, everyone gathering around.

Bishop Whatever's the matter?

Mayor While our party has been going on – the entire place has been looted!

Bishop At Christmas? The monsters!

Mayor They've turned the place topsy-turvy – and taken everything!

Bishop The heathens!

Duchess A robbery?

She looks down. Her jewels have vanished.

Oh no. My diamonds!

Mayor (*to the Duchess*) Come with me. We'll call the police immediately.

Mayor helps Duchess off as Kay spots someone in the crowd.

Kay Your Grace!

Pointing to Charles and Joe.

It's those two men, there, they're –

The Bishop goes after Charles and Joe, caught up in the dance. Peter runs back.
Charles and Joe waltz past and turn to face them. The party turns nightmarish as he makes for the pair, as all the other guests encircle the boys like wolves.

Herne (*off*) Don't lose courage, Kay, even if the wolves are running!

Kay Herne! Where are you? Help us?

Joe lunges for Kay.

Joe The Box!

Charles We've got you now, ha-ha what!

Kay (*presenting the Box*) Hold tight, Peter!

The two boys vanish just in time.

SCENE TEN: IN THE SOUP

The Missionary College. Maria is locked in one of Abner's cells, wearing a hood. Pouncer enters.

Pouncer (*removing Maria's hood*) There is no need to be afraid.

Maria I'm never afraid.

Pouncer Please believe that I speak the truth when I say I admire so much courage in one so young.

Maria I shan't believe a word you ever say again! Raised by nuns! By wolves, more like.

Pouncer If children are pert here, we make them into dog biscuit!

Abner rises through the floor like a devil from hell. Maria shrinks back.

Abner Ladies, ladies! The first word in business is unity . . . let us have unity, or we shall get nowhere. Miss Jones, do we have unity from you?

Maria Never!

Abner Very well. We have a friend in common, a Punch and Judy man, Mr Cole Hawlings.

Maria Yes, he put on a jolly strange show.

Abner But did he give you, or any of your companions, a small shiny box?

Abner puts on his glove.

Maria No . . .

Abner points it at her and twists it in the air . . . she struggles for breath.

Abner Wrong answer!

Maria Please – I can't breathe –

Abner For every wrong answer, it will get harder . . . Did he leave the Box anywhere at Seekings?

Maria (*choking for air*) I don't – know anything – about a stupid – Box of Delights!

Abner gives another sharp twist with the glove. Maria claws at her throat.

Abner A Box of Delights? I don't believe I called it that. Do you, my shining star?

Pouncer I don't recall that you did, my lion.

Maria (*desperate*) Mr Hawlings – mentioned something – his show – don't know – anything else!

Abner The problem, young Miss Maria, is that we believe you do.

Pouncer And we have all the time in the world.

Abner We will see if a further spell in the dark cannot persuade you. If not, then there is always . . .

Pouncer The Scrounger!

Abner and Pouncer laugh as the Scrounger opens up at Maria's feet. He releases the glove, but only so she can scream as she sees a giant underground mincing machine, spewing steam and demonic light . . . The grinding gears drown out her cries as they are all swallowed by darkness.

Kay – with his Box and ship – and Peter – with his chocolate creams – arrive only a few feet away, at the wooded cemetery by the gates to the College.

Peter Do you think we've shaken them off?

Kay For now. The Box wasn't that bad now, was it?

Peter I'm sorry. It's just a bit . . .

Kay Frightening? I know. But is it any more frightening than those wolves?

Peter I don't enjoy going swift through the air at the touch of a button. I don't like to do anything swift, apart from eating chocolate creams.

Kay I don't like this any more than you do, Peter.

A pause while Peter eats another chocolate cream.

Peter Kay . . . I know we're not related . . .

Kay What does it matter if we are or not?

Peter Well, I just wanted to say that if a chap was going to have a brother . . .

Kay You've already got a jolly brave sister, Peter. Whom I'm sure we'll find very soon.

Peter I know. But if I were to have a brother, I think you'd be a very solid one.

Kay Thanks, Peter, you too.

Another chocolate cream . . .

Peter Kay?

Kay Yes, Peter?

Peter Do you think I'm the most tremendous plank?

Kay (*hiding it*) No, not at all . . . not the most tremendous plank, by any means.

Peter But you do still think I'm a plank? I knew it! That's what everyone at school thinks, too. Peter the Plank, they call me.

Kay That's not what I meant –

Wolves howl.

(*Looking around.*) I think the box has bought us to the lake at Hope-under-Chesters. Look – the Missionary College! That's where the vicars who robbed me on the train were headed!

Kay and Peter head for the gate.

Peter It gives me the fantods! I don't like it at all.

Kay I'm going to climb over and search for the others. Coming?

Peter Why don't I . . . stay here and . . . keep a lookout?

Kay It's eight-thirty. If I'm not back by nine, take this track down to Condicote and call for help.

Peter Please don't go! What if they catch you?

Kay Don't worry about me.

Peter Kay?

Kay Now what?

Peter Can I have the Box, just in case?

Kay Sorry, Peter. Better not. Just in case.

Kay climbs over the gate and disappears. Peter left all alone. He dozes off. Then he is woken, by the sound of the Car-o-Plane roaring overhead.

Peter Kay?

Chanting begins, ominous . . . Three hooded monks approach in the mist.

Hello. I think I might be lost.

Charles (*revealing himself*) I think you might be in the soup, ha-ha what!

The monks scrobble Peter – throwing a sack over him. Charles touches a headstone, and a grave opens up – they disappear with Peter, and it closes behind them. Kay reappears over the gate.

Kay Peter? I saw that car aeroplane fly out of the lake! This is where they're keeping Mr Hawlings, I know it! . . . Oh no. Peter! . . . Hello! Anyone?

Only wolves growling in the woods and getting nearer.

Hello . . .

The wolves appear for the first time, encircling Kay.

I have heard you running for a long time. It's all right. I'm ready.

Kay gets out of the Box, shaking. He tries to open it, and the wolves leap – As we snap to black.
   Interval.

Act Two

SCENE ONE: CONDICOTE CAROLS

The Cathedral bells ring out for Christmas Eve!
Teatime on Condicote Town Square.
A crowd of eager spectators await, with stallkeepers offering mulled wine, roasted chestnuts, etc.

Mayor Good evening, everybody! We've all had a terrible shock today with awful robberies at the Bishop's party. Please rest assured that the finest police minds are on the case as we speak.But in the meantime, as we like to say in Condicote, the show must go on.

So without further ado, it's time for the next part of our spectacular thousandth Christmas celebrations in Condicote. I'm delighted to introduce our special carol concert with the Tatchester Cathedral Choir. Please join me in welcoming the Dean, Canon, Rector, Precentor – and the Bishop himself!

The spectators applaud as the Cathedral Choir take up their positions.

Choir (*jubilant*)
Here we come a wassailing,
Among the leaves so green
Here we come a wandering,
So fair to be seen,

Love and joy come to you,
And to your wassail too
And God bless you and send you
A happy new year
And God send you a happy new year!

They are interrupted by a Papergirl cycling on with a copy of The Daily Thriller. *We see the dramatic spinning headlines as she calls them out.*

Papergirl Extra! Extra! Read all about it! Mysterious disappearance in Condicote! Governess at Seekings House and her children missing!

Both Choir and crowd look alarmed, but the Papergirl cycles off.

Choir
God rest you merry, gentlemen,
Let nothing you dismay,
For Jesus Christ our Saviour
Was born upon this day.
To save poor souls from Satan's power,
Which long time had gone astray.
Oh tidings of comfort and joy –

Charles appears, puts a sack over the Dean and scrobbles them!

Comfort and joy
O tidings of comfort and joy.

Papergirl arrives with The Condicote Courier. *The front page appears as –*

Papergirl Mystery deepens! Merry Dean Disappears! Dean of Tatchester Cathedral missing since – (*Checks watch.*) teatime!

The choir looks around warily but keeps going.

Choir
While shepherds watched their flocks by night,
All seated on the ground,
The angel of the Lord came down

Pouncer appears and scrobbles the Canon.

And glory shone around –

Joe emerges from a drain and scrobbles the Rector underground!

(*Very uncertain.*) And glory shone around –

Papergirl returns with The Tatchester Times.

Papergirl Another disappearance! Special! Canon and Rector of Tatchester disappear!

Somebody chucks the Papergirl the latest Musborough Mercury.

Papergirl What clergyman is safe? Murder gang suspected!

Choir
We three kings of Orient are . . .

The Mayor is scrobbled, leaving just the Bishop and the Precentor. Spectators and stallkeepers flee . . . into the arms of wolves.

We *two* kings of Orient are,
Bearing gifts, we traverse afar –

The Precentor is scrobbled. The Bishop is left all on his own.

Papergirl Now half of Condicote vanishes! Mayor of Condicote and council abducted! Citizens flee in fear! European plot suspected! Some fear the Revolution has begun!

Hesitantly, the Bishop sings –

Bishop
Silent night, holy night –

Papergirl Stop press! Startling disappearance of the Bishop of Tatchester!

The Bishop looks confused at this and, flustered, begins again.

Bishop (*querulous solo*)
All is calm, all is bright
Round yon virgin, mother and child –

Wolves have surrounded him.

I see. Not your favourite carol, is it?

The Bishop is scrobbled.

Papergirl Stop press! Prime Minister offers thousand-pound reward for safe return of Bishop of Tatchester and Mayor of Condicote – or Christmas will be cancelled!

An extra-long comedy shepherd's crook around her neck, she's out too.

SCENE TWO: A WITCH

The Missionary College. Many locked doors behind a study area painted with magic symbols, a desk and a chair on a Persian carpet. Pouncer and Charles are plotting.

Pouncer Charles, must you wear that dog collar everywhere you go? It's becoming rather a habit.

Charles Just playing the part, ha-ha what?

Pouncer Don't you ha-ha-what me. What happened to the dark and dangerous jewel thief I hired?

Charles (*taking off his dog collar*) He's still here and just as dark and dangerous.

Pouncer I trust you didn't let Abner know you were coming.

Joe (*entering*) No chance. We waited until the old fool had gone for his morning dip in the lake and then hot-footed it here. He won't even notice we're gone. Not with everything else going on.

Pouncer What do you mean? What's happened?

Joe I don't like this, Pounce. Not a bit. Scrobbling clergy, women and children. Why can't we stick to nicking jewels? It won't come to any good.

Pouncer Don't you think I know it? Not for the first time, Abner Brown has promised me treasure. Yet all I get is incessant moaning about his wretched Box.

Charles We was turning over the best houses in London. A guest at the parties of the season. Have a few cheeky cocktails, a dance or two . . . Then slip upstairs while nobody's looking, help myself! And off down the drainpipe while Joe kept the motor running. But now look at me! Scrobbling little nippers. It had better be worth it, Pounce.

Pouncer Have I ever not been worth it, Charlie boy?

Charles Course not . . .

Pouncer Have I ever let you down, my Joe?

Joe I'm not saying that –

Pouncer Why don't you pop your little dog collar back on, get back to playing vicar, and listen to me? I don't care whether Abner tells you both to scrobble every orphan in Britain or the King of Bulgaria. Do exactly as he says. Arouse no suspicion and stick to the plan.

Unseen by plotters, Abner's magic Head rises out of its plinth behind them.

Charles Whatever you say, boss.

He puts on clerical dog collar.

Ha-ha, what?

Beat.

Pouncer Well, what are you waiting for?

Charles and Joe look shiftily at one another.

Charles Nothing . . . it's just that . . . you know you said you were a . . .

Pouncer A what? A woman who knows herself? Surely not the first one you've ever met?

Joe Yeah, that too, but also – that you were a . . .

Pouncer Spit it out!

Joe A witch! You told that rat you were a witch.

Charles A practiser of the Dark Arts.

Pouncer I did.

Charles Is that what you'll do? Use your magic on him? Otherwise, I don't know how we'll get them jewels back. He keeps them under lock and key in his vault.

Pouncer (*grabbing him by the dog collar*) Do I not look like a witch?

Charles Yeah, but . . .

Pouncer Do I not sound like a witch?

Joe Sure, only . . .

Pouncer And do I not act like a witch?

Charles *and* **Joe** All the time!

Pouncer Precisely. I am known in underworld circles, from the East End of London to the backstreets of Chicago, as – 'The Witch!' But know this, my little vicars. The only dark art I ever learned was the art of the heist. The only thing I'm magic with is this! (*Pulls out her gun.*) And the greatest trick I ever pulled was casting a spell over that creep Abner Brown. But when the time is right –

She drags a finger across her throat.

Charles *and* **Joe** We will get our swag?

Pouncer We will get our swag! And who knows what is in this Box? I suspect that this Box may be the greatest treasure of all. So go, my pretty vicars! Find out what you can. Abner will never reveal it to me. He fears my powers too much.

Charles *and* **Joe** Your wish is our command, wicked witch!

We hear wolves approach . . .

Joe He's back from the lake!

Pouncer So be gone!

They slip into the darkness as Abner appears with a felt jewel bag . . . But he is not alone! Tiny Kay follows, unobserved.

Abner (*to a locked cell door*) Aha! And how is the dear Bish? Are you ready to tell me where my Box is yet?

Bishop (*through grille*) I tell you, rascal, we don't know about any box! Let us go!

Abner clicks his fingers, and doors fling open. We see the Bishop, Mayor, Duchess, Caroline Louisa and Ellen, Cole, Maria, Peter . . . all in their cupboard-sized cells.

Abner (*to the Duchess*) What about you, dear Duchess? Look, here I have your pretty diamonds, which my wolves stole.

He tips the sack into his hand, revealing glittering gems.

Duchess You thief! Those are family heirlooms. Priceless. Give them back. I'll pay you. Whatever you want. Seventy thousand!

Abner Not for seventy million, my dear Duchess, unless you can give me my Box?
 (*To Caroline Louisa.*) That's only fair isn't it, Caroline Louisa? Will you tell me about the Box? You must know all about it.

Caroline Just let the children go, you monster! They have done you no harm. They're innocent.

Abner (*to Cole*) Innocent? So when I open this sluice . . . Great Master Hawlings, shall we see if they float? What will you do with your precious elixir? Live in this hole for eternity? Or sell me my Box for your freedom?!

Cole I will never bargain with you, Abner Brown. I defy you!

Abner Very well. Then you leave me no alternative. Christmas is cancelled!

Mayor But what about our special thousandth Christmas celebration in Tatchester? We were going to have fireworks!

Abner Tonight, there will be no more fireworks! No more special midnight services! No more Condicote! Soon, I, Abner Brown, will open the sluice and let all the water from the lake above down upon your heads. Midnight will strike on the Cathedral clock – and on you all!

Abner clicks his fingers again. The cell doors slam shut. He looks around, making sure he is not watched. He circles his hand in the air over the bronze Head as he mutters a spell:

O ancient head of long ago . . .
O voice of ages past . . .
All-seeing, all-powerful . . .
Answer my command!

Magic begins as the bronze Head twists into life.

Head I am your Head and answer your command!

Abner And what have you seen? Tell me!

Head When will you release me from your spell?

Abner When you have done all that I command! Tell me what you have seen, insolent creature.

Head Your wolves conspire against you. They seek your treasure.

Abner What? Impossible.

Head Speak to the one called . . . Joe. See for yourself. (*Summoning voice.*) Joe!

Joe appears, suddenly summoned – and dazed, trapped in a magic beam of light.

Joe All right, chief!

Abner I hear you wolves have been criticising my orders.

Joe Us? We just wish you'd tell us more about this blooming box of yours.

Abner Tell me, Joe, have you ever heard of Ramon Lully, the famous medieval magician?

Joe Can't say I have, boss – unless he plays down Brixton Music Hall.

Abner (*sighs*) And how about Arnold of Todi? Have you heard of him?

Joe Oh yeah, Arnold of Todi. He runs that upmarket hair salon in Pimlico. Very 'à la mode'.

Abner He does not run a flaming hair salon in Pimlico! He, too, was a sorcerer of the Middle Ages. A very great one. Some might say the greatest . . .

Abner points to a picture. A thirteenth-century wise man looking oddly familiar . . .

Who do you think this is?

Joe It's that old geezer we scrobbled, Cole Hawlings!

Abner Looks just like him. But what does the name say below?

Joe (*reads*) 'Ramon . . . Lully.' You mean –

Abner They're one and the same! Exactly. And when was this picture painted? Oh . . . 1287!

Joe 1287? He's getting on a bit to be touring a Punch and Judy show around the provinces.

Abner He has an Elixir of Eternal Life! Which is why he still plagues my every move! Now, look at this one.

Another period portrait of a more sinister figure, with sharp eyes and a forked beard.

Joe He's the very spit of you, chief. (*Realises.*) You're Arnold . . . of Todi. The hairdresser!

He sees Abner's face.

... The sorcerer. Blimey! You must have been around for hundreds of years.

Abner I was the greatest villain of every age! Until I arrived in this wondrous century of aeroplanes, movies, and machine guns. Only for that wretch Ramon to catch up with me at a fair – and steal my Box using a cheap trick. But I must have it back by midnight tonight – by Christmas!

Joe Why, is it a present for someone?

Abner No, you laughable lowlife. By the laws of magic, without my box, I will be sent back to my own time.

Joe I see! You're kidnapping half of Condicote to ensure that Christmas doesn't happen. Which means you can't get sent back. Then . . . you'd be unstoppable!

Abner Finally, he sees the light.

Joe I still don't like it, boss. Charlie and me . . . we used to be just a simple criminal outfit . . . That's an honest man's game. But all this magic . . . it gives me the shivers, it does.

Abner You don't believe in magic, do you, Joe?

Joe Not half! Not from Ramon or Cole, whoever he is, or you neither . . . Arnold.

Abner That's funny.

Joe Why so?

Abner Because magic doesn't believe in you either. Betray me, would you? My Head never misses a trick. It tells me everything.

The Scrounger opens up, a glowing red pit of grinding terror.

Joe No, no . . . not – the Scrounger!

Wolves drag him in with a roar of machinery and mangled cries.

Abner What's that? Take your time . . .

He laughs cruelly. Tiny Kay gasps and slips, knocking a book off.

Hello!

Abner picks up the book, looking around suspiciously. Tiny Kay freezes. Abner flings open the study door to reveal Pouncer, listening . . .

Pouncer (*cowering, shaken*) Abner! My . . . shield and star, do come to, er, breakfast. The kippers are getting cold.

Abner (*not fooled*) For you, my hell and glory, I would do anything. Anything.

Abner leaves, taking Pouncer firmly by the arm.

SCENE THREE: THE SECRET OF THE BOX

Abner's cells under the Missionary College. Tiny Kay searches for his friends, finding Maria first.

Kay Maria!

Maria You took your time. Were you planning to rescue me this Christmas or next?

Kay I spied on Abner in his study. I know why he scrobbled half of Condicote. He's trying to cancel Christmas.

Maria Cancel Christmas? What a genius. That's the best idea anyone's had since they invented the electric guitar.

Kay No, Maria, don't you see? If he can stop Christmas from happening, and get the Box – then he will be unstoppable. All powerful and immortal.

Maria I'll give him a kick in the shins that will be immortal, all right.

Kay Is Peter here? I think they scrobbled him at the college gates.

Maria In the cell next door.

Peter appears in his cell.

Kay Peter!

Peter Hello Kay.

Kay Thank goodness you're all right!

Peter It's not so bad. This cell is slightly more comfortable than my room at boarding school.

Kay I shouldn't have left you.

Peter It's not your fault. I'm such a plank, aren't I? Letting myself get scrobbled like that?

Kay No, Peter, you're not a plank at all. I think you're very brave.

Maria Brave? The only brave thing he's done is ask for extra gruel.

Peter Kay, I don't fancy Christmas in this tiny underground prison. There's absolutely nowhere to put up a tree.

Maria What are you going to do? What about that Box of yours?

Kay I can't rescue you or defeat Abner alone, even with the Box.

Maria Phooey. If anyone could rescue us, it would be you.

Peter For once, I agree with my sister.

Kay I wish I could be so sure.

Maria But don't you see, Kay? Why old Mr Hawlings gave you the Box and not me or Pudding Face next door?

Kay Why?

Maria Because you're a dreamer, Kay. And maybe that Box might make a dream or two come true.

Kay You truly think so?

Maria I truly think so. As does Peter.

Peter Do I? . . . Oh yes, jolly good show, Kay. You'll sort us out!

Kay In that case . . .

He opens the Box, and Maria and Peter disappear. Kay, back to full size, is in a magic, liminal space of his own.

Herne! All my friends are captured, and Mr Hawlings, too. I am trying to keep you safe, but the wolves are running me close. No one else will help. Show me how to bring an end to this.

Herne appears – softer this time, in a snowy winter pelt.

Herne You know what you have to do, Kay Harker.

Kay No! No, I don't! I could go forward in time, couldn't I, with this Box? To Christmas, this year or next, when we are all together again. To any time. Any time would be better.

Herne Is that what you truly want? Time is a vast book with many pages. Tell me the time you would like to travel to the most.

Kay I don't know.

Herne Perhaps today, Christmas Eve, six years ago?

Kay I want to forget. Don't you see?

Herne conjures a ghostly version of Kay's old home.

My old home . . . don't make me live through this again, please, Herne!

Mr and Mrs Harker appear – as in their photo from before.

I was only reading a book. And should have been paying more attention. So I didn't notice the log –

The fire flares up, consuming them.

I can't help it. It's true what my teachers say at school – and Caroline Louisa, Maria and Peter. I'm just a wretched dreamer.

Herne But dreams are power, Kay. Has the Box taught you nothing?

Kay It has only reminded me – that I let the fire kill my mother and father. Can I stop it?

Herne The Box allows you to travel through time, Master Kay, but you must never change it.

Kay Then what is the point? Why did you show me again? Did you think I had forgotten? When I think about it every single day?

Herne No, Kay. I wanted you to look. You weren't looking.

Kay What am I looking for?

Herne The truth, Kay.

Kay opens the Box again, lost in the glow, watching the scene again and again –

Kay Wait, what's that on the roof? This I haven't seen before. Something in the dark!

He slams the lid shut, trembling.

Herne What is it, Kay? What did you see?

Kay Something I can never forgive.

Herne Now you know the true danger of this Box. What it can make people do. I'm sorry you had to see that.

Kay No, Herne. Now I know what I have to do. Box – take me swift to . . . Abner Brown!

SCENE FOUR: GIVE ME A STORM!

Sacks of jewels are piled on Abner's desk, waiting to fill the empty strong box standing by it. But first, he has business with the Head.

Abner The hour grows late! Christmas is nearly upon us, and still no Box. I can no longer trust my mortal accomplices.

Tiny Kay appears and finds a hiding place.

Tell me, Head, what do you see?

Head Your wolves have captured every single priest and servant from the Cathedral. The Mayor, town council and half of Condicote are in your cells.

Abner So their Christmas celebration is cancelled?

Head No. The citizens of Condicote and Tatchester are determined. It will go ahead. The greatest celebration ever.

Abner Impossible!

Head They have telephoned every church in the country for volunteers. They have sent telegrams requesting urgent help from the authorities.

Abner Then we must stop them! Send demons to cut all the Tatchester telephone lines and telegraph wires!

The Head shakes, muttering. Bat-faced demons explode out of the shadows and scatter to do her bidding, exhausting her.

Head It is done.

Abner And will that stop them?

Head No, friends of the Cathedral are on their way already. Volunteers from every county. Spectators from across the country.

Abner Curse them, and curse you! Dislocate all traffic around Tatchester for twenty miles, so the roads are blocked. Jam the railway points.

Head This is too much magic! Even for you!

Abner Block the traffic, Head, unless you want to stay on that pedestal forever!

The Head shudders with the effort but mutters a spell.

Abner Well?

Head (*exhausted*) They can still come by air. The government in London is putting soldiers on aeroplanes.

Abner Summon a storm to bury them in snow!

Head I will not take innocent human lives.

Abner I made you! Do as I command.

Head Release me first. You promised! It is time.

Abner It is time you learned some respect.

The Head screams as Abner forces her half down into the plinth.

So be it. You are all in mutiny against me. But you forget one thing. I am still the greatest sorcerer who ever lived.

Abner puts on his magic glove and enters spell-casting mode as he uses it to summon the deepest, darkest magic.

Give me a storm from the North, East, South, and West! Flood the countryside with the deepest snow since the wolves first ran! Make the drifts eight feet deep around the Cathedral door! Cancel Christmas and bury them all!

Snow spirals from nowhere, rising to a howling blizzard, threatening to devour everything.

So now, everything is done. Tell me, Head – will I have the Box today?

Head (*muffled*) It will be . . . under your hand.

Abner Who will bring me the Box?

Head A child. It will come under your hand.

Abner A child! Finally! Farewell, Head. You can mend your manners in this rock for eternity.

He squashes her fully into the plinth with the gloved hand – she disappears with a gurgling cry.

After centuries, old Ramon . . . Cole . . . whatever your name is – past, present and future, all is mine! No child or saint can stop me now! Bring me Pouncer!

The blizzard hurls Pouncer into the room before abating.

Pouncer (*bewildered*) . . . Abner. My sultan.

Abner My Angel of Death, here is what you have been waiting for.

Abner empties the sack of diamonds onto the table.

The dear Duchess's rubies . . . worth thirty thousand if they are a penny! These emeralds must be at least twenty. And how about my darling pearls? So light to carry and yet worth so much. Fifty thousand for these beauties, I think! And not to mention the sapphires. There must be three hundred thousand pounds in here alone.

Pouncer Only because your thieves have worked so hard. Thieves who want to see their share. Those of us that are still alive.

Abner Ah yes, poor dear Joe. He lacked the magic touch, didn't you think? But patience, my deadly nightshade. Soon, that Box will be mine once more. Then, together, you and I will have all the riches and power in the world.

In trying to evade him, Tiny Kay drops the Box into the trunk – it sparkles.

Tiny Kay (*to himself*) The Box! I've lost the Box!

Abner What's that?

Abner gets out his magic glove, looking for the noise.

Pouncer Nothing but the wind. I fear all this missing Box has done is make you paranoid, Abner Brown.

Abner (*searching*) Strange, that boy Kay Harker came into my mind just now.

Now, my pearly princess of a pilot, prepare the Car-o-Plane for our imminent departure.

Pouncer You promise you will bring my . . . the . . . jewels directly?

Abner Once I have the Box and those churchy fools in our cellars have been disposed of, I will bring you the jewels directly.

He locks the jewels away in the trunk. Pouncer comes closer to him and lifts the key from his pocket during the following.

Pouncer You swear?

Abner Upon my mother's grave.

Pouncer I thought your mother was a demon?

Abner Precisely. I dare not cross her name, even in death.

Pouncer How very prudent. Very well. I shall see that your flying chariot awaits, my emperor.

She leaves.

Abner Farewell, my Temptress of Time. You'll never see me or a single one of these diamonds again.

He leaves the other way. Tiny Kay is looking for the Box when Pouncer sneaks back in – with Charles!

Pouncer Did I not promise you, Charlie boy? Here is our swag! The jewels we stole – all locked up in his trunk and ready to go in the Car-o-Plane.

Charles He's double-crossed us, Pounce!

Pouncer Luckily, Abner Brown is not as good a thief as I.

Pouncer produces the key she stole, then unlocks the trunk to reveal the jewels.

The Duchess's rubies . . . diamonds, pearls . . . even the special sapphires!

Charles Wave goodbye to Uncle Abner, my little sparklers!

They stuff the lot into holdalls.

Pouncer (*checking trunk*) Not even one worthless piece of glass shall we leave him . . . Wait a moment, though! What's that?

He picks up the shrunken Box.

Charles It's nothing. Just a spare ring box.

Pouncer (*pocketing it*) Might as well add it to the collection.

Tiny Kay She's taken the Box!

Pouncer I wish I could see the old fathead's face when he discovers his loss. But for now – to the Car-o-Plane!

Charles I'll distract Abner by releasing the prisoners.

They head for the cells, followed by Tiny Kay . . .

SCENE FIVE: THE WATER IS A-ROARING IN

Tiny Kay arrives in Abner's underground complex of cells and tunnels but has to hide immediately as –

Tiny Kay Abner!

Abner returns in full flying kit and opens Cole's cell with a click of his fingers.

Abner Now Cole, or Ramon, my merry old soul. In the spirit of past times, I give you one last chance.

He hauls him out. They face each other one last time.

I am ready to fly. My enemies are in chains, Christmas is cancelled, and I have my jewels. All I need now is my Box, and our little competition will be decided once and for all. The greatest sorcerer ever, for eternity. So where is it?

Cole Nothing you can say, in this time or the next, will induce me to give that Box back to you . . . Arnold!

Abner You realise the alternative? Sluices will flood these ancient cellars with thirty feet of water from the lake above. I don't think even your precious elixir will save you from that.

Cole I will let no weakness of mine preserve your evil.

Abner You still refuse? I will have the Box today, anyway. My Head told me I would have it, and the Head never lies.

Cole No, the Head never lies.

Abner What do you mean?

Cole The Box shall not be yours, whatever happens to me. And neither shall you have your jewels.

Abner You ramble in your dotage. Do you know what this lake above us is famous for?

Cole A very ugly scoundrel living on it?

Abner No, for the fool who drowned like a rat in its waters.

With his glove, Abner makes the sluice wheel turn magically of its own accord. A mechanical groan, a gurgle of pipes and distant explosion of released water.

Do you hear? The sluice works beautifully. Thirty feet of water rushing to drown you all – clergy, children, and you! Farewell, Cole, I shan't remember you . . .

Abner blows him a kiss and departs. The water enters as Kay rushes over.

Tiny Kay Mr Hawlings! Mr Hawlings!

Cole (*looking down*) I wouldn't keep that size if I were you, Master Harker.

Tiny Kay I've lost the Box! So now I can't return to normal size.

Cole But the water is a-roaring in, and I'm all locked up.

Tiny Kay Is that it, then? Is Abner Brown going to win?

Cole The wolves have run us very close, haven't they? But do you remember that time at Seekings? When they got as near . . . and yet I got away?

Tiny Kay The painting! But . . .

He looks around.

Cole There is no painting by your father here in this watery cave. You are quite right. But do you have imagination, Kay?

Tiny Kay Caroline Louisa says I have too much imagination.

Cole No such thing! And can you draw, like your father?

Tiny Kay A bit, but I'm not nearly as good . . . Oh Mr Hawlings, the water, it's coming in!

Cole Then let us hope you are a quick artist.

Tiny Kay I have nothing to draw with.

Cole Now, perhaps the wind will settle a little in favour of a travelling man . . .

Cole magics a drawing pad and pencil out of thin air – and hands them to him.

Tiny Kay What should I draw, Mr Hawlings?

Cole What was the last truly beautiful thing you saw?

Tiny Kay (*thinks*) I know! My toy boat, the one the Bishop gave me! *Captain Kidd's Fancy*!

Cole That will do us nicely.

As Tiny Kay draws, the water draws nearer and nearer.

Do not heed the waters, Master Kay. Think of your father and mother; how we will avenge them still.

Tiny Kay (*finishing his sketch*) I think that's the best drawing I've ever done. Can I keep it?

Cole You can do more than keep it. Look what you've done, Kay, you and your imagination.

The sketch becomes a magic vision of a boat, which then becomes a real boat.

Tiny Kay I can't leave you!

Cole Don't mind me, Master Harker – now go while you still can!

Tiny Kay No! Mr Hawlings! Please –

He disappears beneath the waves as Tiny Kay is alone, adrift in his boat.
  Then, over the roaring water, he hears behind him, from the cells:
  The prisoners sing as the boat rises in the water, sails unfurling.

Prisoners
Abide with me: fast falls the eventide;
The darkness deepens;
Lord, with me abide.
When other helpers fail, and comforts flee,
Help, of the helpless, O abide with me!

We see Caroline Louisa, Ellen, the Mayor and the Bishop struggling to stay afloat.

Ellen Help! Help!

He sails to them, and she clambers on board.

Caroline Ellen, can you climb in?

Ellen (*dry as ever*) Yes I can.

Caroline Well then, will you?

She does, along with the Mayor, Duchess and Bishop, as Peter swims alongside the boat.

Tiny Kay Peter!

Peter I tried to swim for it . . . like when I was a trout . . . but I seem to have lost the knack.

Peter shows Tiny Kay he has found the Box. It hums.

Tiny Kay The Box, Peter, the Box! How did you get it?

Peter That thief, Pouncer, ran past my cell with a sack of jewels, laughing, so I stuck my foot out and tripped her up. She picked up the jewels . . . but left this behind.

Tiny Kay Bravo, Peter!

He gives Tiny Kay the Box, and he then transforms to full size.

Caroline Kay. How did you find us?

Kay You remember that fellow who gave us a Punch and Judy show?

Peter Mr Hawlings! Is he alive?

Kay I don't know . . . the water pulled us apart.

Caroline You spoke of him several times, and I didn't believe you. I'll never not believe your stories again, Kay. I'm so sorry.

Maria (*off*) Help! Help! Kay!

Kay Maria! I'll go back for her.

Caroline Kay, absolutely not. It's far too dangerous.

Kay I'm sorry, Caroline Louisa. We'll be home for Christmas.

Caroline Oh Kay. My dear child. Do you promise?

Kay With all my heart. Box, take me swift to Maria!

With a flash, the boats of rescued prisoners disappear as . . .

SCENE SIX: TOODLE-OO!

... The Box brings Kay to one side of the underground river. Abner is high on the other side, holding a struggling Maria tight.

Kay Abner! I am no longer afraid of you. Because I have this!

He holds up the Box.

Abner My Box! Under the hand of a child, indeed. Give it to me this instant, or this minx dies a cold and cruel death.

Maria Don't do it, Kay. I'm all right. Well, I can't swim, but apart from that, I'm all right.

Kay You can't swim?

Maria Look, I can reassemble a pistol in under fifteen seconds. I never said I was perfect!

Kay I'll get you out of this, I swear.

Abner Ha! If you think that, then you have learned nothing!

Kay But you're wrong, Abner Brown. I have learned that this Box is a beautiful, magical thing. It has shown me – shown us all – the wonders of the world.

Maria It made me like being a duck! Even though I can't swim. (*To Abner.*) So there! I'm not scared of you after all!

Abner Pathetic! (*To Kay.*) You are just a little schoolboy deceived by some old man he met on a train.

Kay The only person who has been deceived is you. You were told you would have the Box under your hand. And you did, earlier, in your vault. But I was so little you never even noticed.

Abner Give it to me. Now.

Abner dangles Maria over the water, and she cries out in fear.

Kay No.

Kay holds Box out over the water. It glows and shudders.

Abner You wouldn't dare.

Maria He jolly well would. Chuck it, Kay!

Kay Herne showed me. Christmas, six years ago. Your magic Head had told you that a boy called Kay Harker would one day use your Box against you. So, you burned our house down. You killed my parents.

Abner Yes! What of it? They were nothing to me. And here we are. I have won. Now give me the Box, or I shall kill your little friend, too.

Maria Don't do it, Kay!

Kay (*quietly*) Sorry, Maria, but I'm not afraid of you anymore. I like you . . . I really like you. And don't want to lose you. (*Bold.*) I don't want to lose anyone ever again.

Kay lobs the Box over the water to Abner. It sails through the air, showering light like a comet. Abner catches the Box, triumphant with glee.

Above, Abner opens the box, filling his face with a demonic light.

Abner My Box! My sweet, sweet precious Box. How I have missed you! You lose, Ramon Lully! I am the greatest magician, after all!

Kay Now let her go!

Abner Very well.

Abner drops Maria into the water, which rises still higher. Maria sinks into the watery gloom.

Kay No! Maria!

Kay dives in to grab her, but she has vanished beneath the waves.

He dives back down, frantic – but it's no good. She's gone.
An eerie sound and light as the Box prepares to transport Abner.

Kay (*resurfacing*) You murderer! You've killed her!

Abner So I have. Toodle-oo!

He waves . . . as the Car-o-Plane comes to him! Out of the darkness!

Pouncer (*voice-over*) Oh Abner, you old rogue, did you truly think you could diddle Sylvia Pouncer? We have stolen all your treasures! Every last gem.

Charles And this is for Joe, ha-ha what!

The plane dive-bombs/drops a sandbag on Abner, who tumbles into the water, dropping the Box as he does.

Toodle-oo, old chap!

And they fly off to freedom as Abner writhes before sinking to his death. The Box bobs on the surface. Exhausted as he is, Kay can just reach it, and –

Kay Box! Take me swift to Maria!

We head underwater as the Box brings him to the river depths – and Maria.
Kay dives to rescue his friend but cannot simultaneously hold her and the Box.
His final choice.
He lets the open Box sink and grabs Maria.
Her eyes open, and their fingers touch – with one last flash, the Box of Delights shuts and sinks into the watery shadows, lost to time and space forever . . .

SCENE SEVEN: LIONS AND UNICORNS

The snow-covered edge of the lake by the Missionary College, the moon and stars glowing in the sky above.

Caroline Where are Kay and Maria? We can't just leave them down there.

Peter Should we call the police?

Mayor I fear we may be too late to stop that villain –

Maria appears from underground with Kay.

Maria Have no fear! That villain is dead! Kay defeated him!

Peter Maria! Kay! You're alive!

He hugs her.

Wait – who have you hurt this time?

Maria No one! This time, Kay did all the hurting. He was magnificent!

Kay (*to Maria*) I couldn't have done it without you.

A moment.

Caroline Children! I don't know what to say. Leaving the house at night without permission. Putting yourselves in terrible danger. Not to mention . . . swimming in your smart clothes!

Kay Are you cross, Caroline Louisa?

Caroline Cross? My dearest Kay – Maria – Peter – I couldn't be more proud! We shall be together for Christmas after all.

Maria Ugh. I loathe happy endings.

Bishop But what happened to that evil rascal Abner Brown?

Cole steps out of the snowy woods with Barney.

Cole He has been swept deep into the caves by the flood. I don't think any man will find part of him again.

Peter Mr Hawlings!

Kay How did you – Never mind.

He realises he will never get a straight answer to this question. And hugs him instead.

You're alive!

A distant clock chimes eleven.

Mayor Your Grace! It's gone eleven!

Bishop Mayor. You must get me, my clergy and these heroic children to Tatchester Cathedral in time for our thousandth Christmas celebration!

Mayor Impossible, Your Grace. We will never get through the snow.

Bishop Then there will be no service and no Christmas!

Cole I would not be so sure, Your Grace. A travelling man can often find a way, can he not, children?

Children He can!

Cole We needn't give up hope yet. Listen . . . Is that . . . sleigh bells?

Mayor Why, I believe it's Father Christmas, children!

Maria Phooey. If Father Christmas ever comes down our chimney, he'd better be ready for the gunfight of his life.

Kay It's not Father Christmas, though . . .

Herne flies across the moon in her sleigh driven by lions and unicorns . . .

Maria Herne! Good-oh! And her sleigh is driven by lions and unicorns, which I far prefer to reindeer.

Peter Herne, I would keep those lions away from those unicorns if I were you!

With a roar from the lions, Herne lands in her sleigh.

Herne Get in, everyone. I can take you in my sleigh.

They board the sleigh, which departs with bells and roars.

Choir
Ding dong merrily on high,
In heav'n the bells are ringing.
Ding dong! Verily the sky
Is riv'n with angel singing.
Gloria, Hosanna in excelsis!
Gloria, Hosanna in excelsis!

SCENE EIGHT: THE OIL OF ETERNITY

Back to Tatchester Cathedral for Christmas – just as the clock strikes a quarter to midnight!
A congregation of rescued clergy, choir, children and citizens. But the famous stained glass windows are dark . . .

Bishop We are just in time . . . but where are the lights?

Kay Abner Brown's magic head cut the electricity!

Bishop Quick – everyone, more candles!

Cole and Kay are left together as the Bishop leads others to light the candles.

Cole There may be a quicker way. You see that tripod there, Kay . . .

They move to a large church tripod.

Here is that bottle Abner Brown wanted nearly as much as his Box.

Kay The Elixir of Life!

Cole The very same that Alexander the Great found burning in the desert. The Oil of Eternity. I took it for an elixir many a year ago. But now my race is run, and its purpose served. This Feast of Nativity is saved.

He shows Kay the bottle.

Look here. There is but a drop left. I give it to you, Kay Harker, I give it to you all, and I give it to Christmas!

Cole throws the last drop of oil on the tripod. A blast of supernatural light dazzles the congregation, fading to a festive candlelit glow behind the stained glass. But where Cole stood, only a hat and pile of clothes remain.

(*Off.*) May it burn for the rest of time!

The clock strikes twelve, and we hear fireworks outside.

Kay Thank you, Mr Hawlings! And Merry Christmas!

Bishop Merry Christmas, everyone!

Cheers erupt in reply. Then, the moment freezes, fading into the past as we wake from the dream, as the Choir sings:

Choir
I saw three ships come sailing in
On Christmas Day, on Christmas Day
I saw three ships come sailing in
On Christmas Day in the morning

And all the bells on earth shall ring
On Christmas Day, on Christmas Day
And all the bells on earth shall ring
On Christmas Day in the morning.

SCENE NINE: SLEEPERS, WAKE

Christmas Eve, now. Back where we began, in Seekings attic.
  Kay wakes up as if from a trance, still holding the toy train. Grandad steps out of the shadows.

Kay And was that all a dream? Did any of it happen, Grandad? Or was it just a story?

Grandad You tell me.

Kay It felt so real! Like I was fighting wolves . . . saving the Box!

Grandad Dreams can be powerful, Kay – I told you. They are how change always begins.

Kay I know that now.

Pause.

Do you still miss them . . . your parents?

Grandad Every day. But here I am.

Kay You mean . . . with Mum . . . and Dad . . . Christmas will be all right again?

Grandad Maybe this year will be different. Perhaps the one after that, too. But in the end, I promise, Christmas will be all right again.

Kay Thanks, Grandad.

Pause.

And if the wolves run?

Grandad You will know what to do!

Kay Without magic, though . . .

Grandad It is not magic alone you need to beat the wolves. But hope, bravery and . . . a little imagination!

He produces an antique glass vial, which sparkles.

Kay The elixir! What you were looking for –

Grandad It's quite empty, I'm afraid . . . but I kept the vial all this time. The last remaining piece of Mr Hawlings' magic. To remind me.

Kay What?

Grandad Something you must promise me you'll never forget, Kay. Nothing is ever truly lost.

The dream memories of Box world allies emerge from the shadows – Caroline, Maria, Peter, Barney – unforgotten.

Only reborn in another form.

Kay opens the vial.

Those we love are taken from us time and time again.

The Phoenix magically appears out of it –

(*Off.*) But look – the beauty of their memory never fades.

Kay watches the Phoenix burn to a ball of flame . . . a single spark . . . and then to black.
   The End.